THE
TODDLER
SURVIVAL GUIDE

COMPLETE PROTECTION
FROM THE WHINY UNFED

MIKE & HEATHER SPOHR

VOYAGEUR
PRESS

Brimming with creative inspiration, how-to projects, and useful information to enrich your everyday life, Quarto Knows is a favourite destination for those pursuing their interests and passions. Visit our site and dig deeper with our books into your area of interest: Quarto Creates, Quarto Cooks, Quarto Homes, Quarto Lives, Quarto Drives, Quarto Explores, Quarto Gifts, or Quarto Kids.

© 2017 Quarto Publishing Group USA Inc.
Text © 2017 Mike Spohr and Heather Spohr

First published in 2017 by Voyageur Press, an imprint of The Quarto Group,
401 Second Avenue North, Suite 310, Minneapolis, MN 55401 USA.
T: (612) 344-8100 F: (612) 344-8692   QuartoKnows.com

Voyageur Press titles are also available at discount for retail, wholesale, promotional, and bulk purchase. For details, contact the Special Sales Manager by email at specialsales@quarto.com or by mail at The Quarto Group, Attn: Special Sales Manager, 401 Second Avenue North, Suite 310, Minneapolis, MN 55401 USA.

10 9 8 7 6 5 4 3 2 1

ISBN: 978-0-7603-5219-9

Library of Congress Cataloging-in-Publication Data

Names: Spohr, Mike, author. | Spohr, Heather, author.
Title: The toddler survival guide : complete protection from the whiny unfed
  / Mike Spohr, Heather Spohr.
Description: Minneapolis : Voyageur Press, [2017]
Identifiers: LCCN 2016059312 | ISBN 9780760352199 (hardback)
Subjects: LCSH: Child rearing--Humor. | Toddlers--Humor. | Parenting--Humor.
  | BISAC: HUMOR / Topic / Marriage & Family. | FAMILY & RELATIONSHIPS /
  Parenting / Fatherhood. | FAMILY & RELATIONSHIPS / Parenting / Motherhood.
Classification: LCC PN6231.C315 S64 2017 | DDC 649/.10207--dc23
LC record available at https://lccn.loc.gov/2016059312

Acquiring Editor: Thom O'Hearn
Project Manager: Alyssa Bluhm
Art Director: James Kegley
Page Designer: Amelia LeBarron
Cover Illustrator: James Kegley
Interior Illustrator: Ted Slampyak
Layout: Erin Fahringer

Printed in China

TABLE OF CONTENTS

INTRODUCTION

Raising a toddler and surviving a zombie attack may not seem like very similar experiences, but they're actually much more alike than you realize. Toddlers and zombies both communicate mainly through groans. They clumsily trail after you everywhere you go (even into the bathroom). And—upon entering your life—both zombies and toddlers will leave you frazzled, on edge, and deeply sleep deprived.

If you've picked up this book it's likely because you have, or will soon have, a toddler. We have some very bad news for you: the epidemic is worse than you realize. Today's toddlers are far and away the most ill-behaved, unpredictable, and tantrum-prone toddlers in history. This isn't to say historical toddlers didn't have their unruly moments; they most definitely did, and we will touch upon them in this book. But it's safe to say that if you left a modern toddler in a room with a dozen toddlers from the past, all of them would be crying within a matter of minutes except for the kid in the *Frozen* T-shirt.

So, what happened to turn toddlers from mild irritants into adorable little nightmares capable of breaking a babysitter in less than twenty minutes? The cause of this seismic shift in behavior is one of the most hotly debated topics in the scientific community, with everything from global warming to fast food consumption to blame. As scientists race to determine the cause and find a cure, they are heartened by the fact that (at least for now) this abhorrent behavior is limited to toddlerhood. (Should it extend by years into the future, it could spell doom for all of humankind.)

Until that dark day, however, the biggest problem caused by this behavioral scourge is that it has made living with toddlers incredibly difficult. *The Toddler Survival Guide* is a handbook to help you survive these challenging times. We saw the need for such a book as we have not only survived these trying years ourselves, we work day in and day out with the parents of toddlers. For more than a decade, we have studied toddlers up-close in their natural habitat.

This book will cover survivor skills including how you can outfit your home to outlast a toddler occupation (baby gate, cabinet locks, wine), how you can subdue an angry toddler ("Elmo's Song," mac and cheese, smartphone), and even how you can safely venture into public together without your toddler (or you) bursting into tears. It is our hope that from these pages you will learn the skills, tools, and mindset needed to successfully handle any encounter with a toddler. We also hope that upon reaching the conclusion of this book you will feel confident enough to stand up and shout, "I will not be a victim of my toddler! I will survive!" (Or at the very least, you will know you're not alone out there.)

There is also a light at the end of the tunnel. Whenever the prospect of living two or more years with a toddler becomes too much to bear, keep in mind that if you can endure it, your child will transition into the comparatively serene (though still somewhat infuriating) preschool years. So, what do you say? Do you have the courage to meet the toddler invasion head on?

PREPARING THE HOME FOR A
TODDLER INVASION

CHAPTER 1

There's no avoiding it: your baby will soon turn into a full-fledged, card-carrying toddler. When this happens, the nice, well-kept home you're so proud of (or perhaps the somewhat messy one that embarrasses you when company unexpectedly drops by) will be a thing of the past. Your home will become a war zone, and like all war zones, it won't be pretty.

You can bar the windows and shut the doors, but it won't do any good. Your toddler will always be right there beside you . . . the screams will be coming from *inside* the house! If you're to have any hope whatsoever of getting to the other side of toddlerhood without seeing your home take a serious dip in value (or without surrendering your deposit) you will need to ready your home as if you were—you guessed it—preparing for war.

ACCEPTING THE NEW NORMAL

You may think you're prepared for what it will be like to have a toddler in the home because you've spent the previous year or so living with a baby, but make no mistake: a baby is not a toddler. Babies are all but immobile for their first several months, and even when they do start crawling, they remain low to the ground. Toddlers, on the other hand, are able to wreak havoc vertically and with velociraptor-like speed. Not only that, but whereas babies spend most of their time thinking about little more than eating, sleeping, and relieving themselves, toddlers can imagine all sorts of mischief but without any of the impulse control that stops older children from doing the especially ill-advised. For these reasons and hundreds more, you must adapt your home to the presence of a toddler. We simply cannot emphasize enough how grave a mistake it would be for you to try to keep things status quo once you have a toddler in your midst. Still don't believe us? Perhaps the testimonials of these parents will change your mind:

> *"Before I became a mother I was very proud of the fact my friends described my home as 'Straight out of Architectural Digest.' I certainly had no intention of redecorating it just because I was pregnant. I was not going to become one of those parents who had toys strewn about and beanbags in the living room. Gag! My home continued to impress after the birth of my son, Alistair, but then one day something about Alistair . . .*

changed. I took him to the pediatrician, who broke the bad news to me: Alistair had become a toddler. That night he ran into the entryway and knocked over my replica statue of David, breaking off its little penis, then swiped a jar of Nutella from the cupboard and used it to finger-paint on my $5,000 Persian rug. It's now nine months later and I have beanbags in every room."

—Amy V., Connecticut

"It used to be that if there were a party, it was at my house. I hosted every wedding shower, every girls' brunch, every Oscars party—everything! My mom told me I would have to start letting my friends host the parties once my daughter, Angie, became a toddler, but I didn't listen. Instead, I planned an epic wedding shower for seventy-five guests. Two minutes before guests started arriving I discovered Angie sitting on the cake I'd commissioned for the event, scooping up the frosting with her dirty little fingers. Later, the guest of honor found a long-lost sippy under the couch that still had milk in it and—upon opening it and taking a whiff—threw up all over the giant bowl of Caesar salad I'd just brought out. Now I only throw parties at my friend Chuck's place (okay, Chuck E. Cheese's)."

—Tamia R., Michigan

"I used to roll my eyes when people said I needed to babyproof my home and think, 'What a waste of time! My mother never babyproofed and I'm still here, aren't I?' Sadly, my refusal to babyproof lead to three costly trips to the emergency room—all for me! Once, because I didn't have a baby gate, I had to dive to stop my toddler, Dylan, from running out of the room and tore my ACL. Another time Dylan and I were playing on the floor when I hit my forehead on the corner of the coffee table and needed twelve stitches. Lastly, I stuck my finger into an outlet and got electrocuted. That one had nothing to do with Dylan—I'd just had too many beers and wondered what would happen—but I sure wish I'd put one of those covers on the outlet."

—Doug M., Oregon

As you can see, the longer you delude yourself that having a toddler won't change your life, the worse things will be for you. Simply put, you must accept the new normal (which is anything but) if you hope to keep your home from falling into condemnable condition.

PROTECTING YOUR HOME

Simply accepting your new normal isn't enough. You also must develop a tactical strategy, and fast. To get an idea of the strain and pressure your home will be under, it's a good idea to re-watch *Poltergeist*, especially the last twenty minutes. The key difference is that, while the damage done to the home in *Poltergeist* was the handiwork of thousands of angry spirits, the damage soon to be done to your home will come courtesy of a single toddler.

The most vulnerable part of your home will be your walls. It doesn't matter how many coloring books or art pads you

buy your toddler, she is not going to be content to contain her scribbling in them. Toddlers are like tiny Banksys who want their work to be seen on the biggest canvas possible, and in your home that canvas is your walls. As if that weren't bad enough, your toddler will have an uncanny ability to "express" herself at the most inopportune times possible.

Taking care of some last-minute cleaning before your easily offended great aunt comes to visit? Your toddler will likely use that time to draw a giant butt on the entryway wall—something your great aunt won't appreciate no matter how tastefully it's done. Similarly, if you get a phone call or accidentally doze off on the couch, you can be sure your toddler will exploit this momentary lapse in supervision by busting out her crayons.

Unfortunately, there isn't much you can do to curb your toddler's drive to draw on the walls. Some parents attempt

TODDLER TIP #1 You can remove toddler-made markings from walls using hair spray, warm water, and a rag.

to discipline their toddlers by making them clean the marks off the walls themselves, but standing there waiting for your toddler to "clean" something is more of a punishment for you than for your toddler. Instead, make a steadfast rule that your toddler is never to use crayons or markers unsupervised, and always collect them the moment she's finished. Basically, the more you think of yourself as a prison guard, the better. Just as prisoners aren't allowed to take utensils out of the cafeteria, your toddler shouldn't be allowed to take crayons out of the family room. You need to remain on high alert, too, because toddlers will scheme to get their hands on contraband just as fervently as a prisoner will. Toddlers, for example, have been known to mule a crayon back from a restaurant and do damage with it later at home. You should also do regular inspections of your home. If you don't, and your toddler finds a half crayon under the couch, you will regret it later.

Another area toddlers can shockingly damage is the bathroom. While toddlers generally resist potty training and want to spend as little time as possible in the bathroom for its intended purpose, they love to just hang out in there for fun. This is not only gross, but sure to end poorly for your bathroom. For example, if you leave a tampon out, your toddler will flush it down the toilet (requiring a very expensive visit from the plumber). She will also pull on the cabinet knobs until they come off and leave the faucet water running (which could end up being every bit as expensive as the visit from plumber in the long run). To limit potential damage, be sure to put any items your toddler could do mischief with (like tampons and plungers) out of her reach, and make a firm rule that she is never allowed in the bathroom by herself.

The rest of the home is not immune to your toddler, of course. While the many ways she could end up damaging your home are too vast to fully catalogue, they nonetheless include turning a light switch on and off until the fuse blows, putting impossible-to-peel-off stickers on your hardwood floors, and cramming fruit snacks into your locks. To combat these attacks, it is wise to always remain on high alert, and to always *try* to stay one step ahead of your toddler.

HEADING OUTSIDE

Considering all of the damage a toddler can do to the inside of your home, we forgive you for thinking, "I know! I'll just keep my toddler outside all day and only bring her inside for diaper changes, naps, and bedtime!" The problem with this plan (besides requiring you to be outside all day too) is that toddlers can also do plenty of damage to the *outside* of your home.

The good news is that if your home rests on a dirt plot that is totally devoid of landscaping, your toddler won't be able to do quite as much devastation (the bad news is that everyone on your street will almost certainly hate you for lowering their resale values). However, if you have landscaping or a garden, you're in for a whole lot of trouble. That's because your toddler won't take into account how expensive the flowers are or how many hours you spent planting them. All she will think upon seeing them is, "Ooh! Pretty!" or "I want to give these flowers to my dolls!" or even "I'm going to pretend I'm Godzilla and stomp through this garden like it's Tokyo!" So, unless you want every flower in your yard picked or flattened in a shockingly short amount of time, you should always stay within a three-second dash of your toddler when outside.

Flowers are by no means the only thing your toddler will destroy. She will also break pots, lawn gnomes, pink flamingos, birdhouses, doghouses, sundials, Greek statues,

RECORDED TODDLER DYSFUNCTION THROUGHOUT HISTORY

In 1940, a French teen stumbled upon the entrance to the Lascaux Cave. Upon exploring the interior, archaeologists found nearly two thousand cave paintings that dated back more than seventeen thousand years. This entry is from the notes of archaeologist Henri-Édouard-Prosper Breuil:

"NOVEMBER 17, 1940
A very curious thing happened today as we moved into a chamber some eighty meters from the entrance. The paintings, which until that point were primarily depictions of large animals, suddenly gave way to a series featuring human figures. At the center of these paintings was what appeared to be a prehistoric child of three or so. In one painting, the child was seized by a fit of anger so disruptive that it alerted an angry rhinoceros to his family's location. In another, the child refused to eat a piece of meat that his exhausted mother had prepared over the fire. In yet another painting, the child could be seen scribbling on the cave walls to his father's horror. Indeed, many of the walls in the area still bear visible defacement in the scrawl of a small child—perhaps the very child depicted in the paintings."

and basically anything else you enjoy having in your yard. Again, staying close to your toddler at all times is the only way to stop these atrocities from happening.

Lastly, you must always check your toddler's feet, hands, and pockets before letting her back inside. Fail to do this and she might not only trail dirt all over your rugs, but also bring a wide variety of bugs, insects, and lizards (or as she will refer to them, "pets") inside. To avoid nearly having a heart attack a week or so later when a lizard runs across your foot, take a cue from Australia. They're incredibly strict about what creatures they let into their country, and you should be too.

PROTECTING YOUR STUFF

The good news is that your toddler probably won't completely destroy your home to the point where it's unsalvageable. The bad news is that it's a totally different story when it comes to your stuff. John Lennon sang, "Imagine no possessions/I wonder if you can." You'll find imagining no possessions pretty easy when you have a toddler because most of your stuff is broken anyways. To avoid having to conduct a funeral for your favorite things every week, you'd better start preparing to go head-to-head with your toddler now.

There are two kinds of possessions you will have to safeguard against your toddler: those you can put away and out of reach, and those you will have no choice but to leave exposed to your toddler. In theory, the things you

TODDLER TIP #2

Make a concerted effort to limit how much you let your toddler use your phone (if at all). This will limit the chances of her dropping it into the toilet, smashing its screen, or texting gibberish to your boss.

can put away and out of reach are the easiest to keep safe, but to do that takes some serious discipline. Let's pretend, for example, that your greatest passion in life—outside of your partner and monstrous little toddler—is playing the ukulele. You can't go a day without strumming your priceless, handmade uke (signed by the late, great Israel "IZ" Kamakawiwoʻole, no less!) without feeling a little shaky. You *need* to play that little wood box, but the sad truth is that if you truly care about it you will stash it on the top shelf of your closet and forget about it until your toddler is older. "Put it away for years?" you're thinking. "That's impossible!" Maybe. But if you don't, the odds are you will accidentally leave it out one day, and when you do, your toddler will use it to do her best Kurt Cobain impression, complete with the guitar smash at the end.

The second kind of possessions—the ones you can't safeguard from your toddler—are much harder to protect. Your couch, for example, is going to be directly in the line of fire (unless you decide to throw a plastic cover over it like you're a senior citizen living in Boca Raton). You can and should do your best to keep the couch clean by banning your toddler from consuming food and drinks on it, but eventually your toddler will: A) have an "accident" on it, B) knock over the coffee you were dumb enough to perch on its arm, C) leave chocolate-covered fingerprints on every cushion, D) use a ballpoint pen to draw an agonizingly large portrait of *Sofia the First*, or E) all of the above plus a whole lot more. Spoiler alert: the answer is "E." Are you cringing at the thought of your couch looking like it spent a generation in a fraternity's game room? Well, you'll also have to get used to the idea of your toddler hurling a block at your flat screen (leaving a permanent streak across it), spilling juice on your computer (frying it for good), and leaving toy cars out to get sucked up into your vacuum.

In the end, your best defense against these ravages is to simply throw up your hands and accept that stuff is going to get broken, destroyed, or ruined, and to soothe yourself with fantasies of the future when you'll no longer have to yell, "This is why we can't have nice things!"

STAYING SAFE

Your toddler isn't only going to come after your stuff; she's going to come after you too. To avoid ending up on a first name basis with the crew down at the emergency ward, you will need to be prepared for all kinds of toddler attacks.

First and foremost, you must be on the lookout for what toddlerologists refer to as "The Flail." Here's how it works: your toddler will move within close proximity of you in a relaxed manner. Then, suddenly and inexplicably, she will violently fling an arm or leg in your direction, nailing you in the nose, neck, or most regrettably, in the crotch. To protect yourself against this savagery, it's a good idea to rest a hand on your toddler's arms and legs during cuddle sessions.

Question: How did you become interested in toddlerology?
Answer: Upon graduating from university, I originally intended to study the lost Pygmy tribes of Uganda, but on a fourteen-hour flight to Kampala I sat behind a terror of a toddler unlike any I had ever seen before. By the time we landed, this incredible specimen had made everyone on the flight irate—even people sitting forty rows ahead who were wearing headphones—and I knew then and there I'd found my true calling.

Q: What does your typical workday look like?
A: Typically, I spend most of my days conducting research in the field. Recently I embedded with a group of toddlers at a McDonald's PlayPlace and was accepted as one of their own. The moment their leader offered me a hardened fry she found on the floor (thus signifying that I had been accepted) was the greatest moment of my career.

Q: Why do you think toddlers have become the way they are?
A: We have seen this kind of rapid evolution in less advanced species, but never in more advanced ones—and certainly not in humans. Toddlers' rapidly increasing acuity for misbehavior is truly alarming, and its cause is still a mystery. My theory (unproven, of course) is that there is something in the fruit snacks.

Q: What do you think the future holds for our toddlers and us?
A: It's possible that within the next ten years, toddlers will develop a super intelligence that allows them to enslave every human on earth over the age of four. But if that doesn't happen I think "My Toddler and Me" music classes will continue to grow in popularity.

The mayhem doesn't end there. Your toddler will run, jump, and dive into you, generally when you're not paying attention. She will pull your hair and ears, pinch your nipples (regardless of whether you're male or female), and scratch your face with her razor-sharp toddler talons. If you wear glasses, she will pull and push on them, injuring the bridge of your nose . . . and your glasses. (Side-note: if you're bespectacled, you should budget now for a new pair of glasses or two.) And, if you try to nap in her presence, she will wake you by hurling herself on top of you. Because of this, it's always best to nap in the fetal position, ideally while covering your face and head with your hands.

Lastly, you need to always be on the lookout for any signs of impending tantrums. Once in full tantrum mode, your toddler will kick and flail with a rage-fueled power that is at least two to three times stronger than that of the non-tantrum variety. Most dangerously, your tantruming toddler will perform the backwards head-butt, dramatically arching her back and flinging her head backwards toward your face. The back of your toddler's skull, when it meets your face at great speed, can easily split a lip or break your nose.

As you have likely figured out by now, fully relaxing in the presence of your toddler is not advisable. This is less than ideal, of course, but if fully relaxing is a priority of yours, parenthood was a very, very poor choice.

PREPARING THE HOME FOR A TODDLER INVASION

PHONES

There's nothing you own that your toddler will want to hold and touch more than your phone. It plays music! It has games! It takes selfies! Yes, a smartphone will be your best friend and your worst enemy. It will keep your kid busy and quiet when you're at a restaurant or talking to adults, but when you give it to your toddler once, she will want it again, and again, and again.

Some people will tell you that letting your toddler play with your phone is bad for her. That is debatable. What isn't debatable is that giving your phone to your toddler is bad for someone else: you. Here are just a few of the ways your toddler can wreak havoc on your life with that little device:

- She will erase apps, videos, images, and emails.
- Her grubby fingers will ruin the camera.
- She will call people—and it will always be someone you absolutely do not want her calling, like your boss.
- She will respond to messages and send voice texts.

TODDLER TIP #3

If someone gives you guff for letting your toddler use your phone, remind them that we live in an information age, and the sooner he understands how to survive in it, the better.

- She will post a woefully low score on a game to your Facebook timeline—and everyone you know will see it.
- She will lock you out of your phone.
- She will drop the phone and shatter the screen.
- She will drop your phone into the toilet, sending it to a watery grave.

Obviously, never giving your toddler your phone is the best line of defense, but that's also the most unrealistic option. Instead, take precautions to protect your phone.

Invest in a sturdy, waterproof case that will guard against water damage and accidental drops. You can also set a password to unlock your phone (but be warned, if a toddler tries too many times to unlock it, you can get locked out for hours). There are even programs that lock your kid into whatever app you want her to play on, preventing her from exploring (and destroying) your phone.

Above all, teach your toddler that while a smartphone may be fun, it's not a toy. Sure, there are a lot of games on it, but it's an expensive, important piece of technology that you rely on for all sorts of different tasks. This might be a tough lesson for a toddler to learn, but eventually she will get it, especially if you take the phone from her the second she does something on it she shouldn't.

PROTECTING YOUR TODDLER FROM YOUR TODDLER

As bad as the toddler-created mayhem discussed thus far may sound, the sad truth is that you won't spend much time worrying about any of it—not the butts scrawled on walls, not the broken heirlooms, and not even the

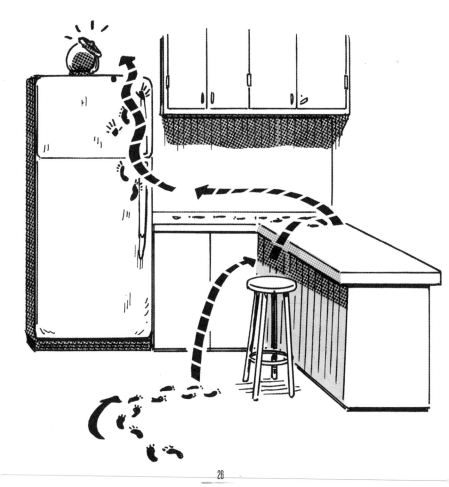

enthusiastic kicks to your groin. What you will worry about is the very real prospect that your toddler's wild ways will cause her to accidentally injure herself. And since you can't put your toddler in a straightjacket for the entirety of her toddlerhood (because it will stunt her development and likely get you arrested), you will need to make toddlerproofing your home a major priority.

Now you may be thinking, "Toddler-proof the house? Why? The place is already baby-proofed." But what you need to understand is that letting a toddler loose in a home that is only baby-proofed is about as prudent as patching up a hole in a parachute with Scotch tape. What makes toddlers such a risk to themselves? They combine increased physical dexterity and an insatiable curiosity with absolutely no sense of self-preservation. This is a very, *very* bad combination.

To toddler-proof your home, you will first need to revisit your baby-proofing. It's probably been a year or so since you did it, so it's a good idea to see how things are holding up. If a drawer or cabinet lock is broken (or even loose), replace it. If an outlet cover is missing, get a new one. And if there are any drawers, cabinets, or outlets that escaped your first round of baby-proofing, think about baby-proofing them now. If this sounds like overkill, remind yourself you

Be careful not to let your toddler see you hide something she desires (like candy) in a high, out-of-reach spot. If she sees you do this, she will make it her mission to climb up to it and possibly hurt herself in the process.

are no longer dealing with a goofy-grinned baby who can only stand if she's holding onto something. Your kid has seriously upped her game, and so should you.

Next, get low on the ground and look at your home from your toddler's perspective. Ask yourself, "If I were a psychotic toddler hell-bent on putting myself at as much risk as possible, what would I do?" Remove any items that make your Spidey senses tingle even a little, and be on the lookout for anything she could pull down on herself. Televisions should be mounted on the wall or secured with a TV anchor.

It is also crucial that you think vertically. Toddlers love to climb things, and will go about it with the temerity of a mountain climber. They will push chairs and stools against counters to climb onto them, and even scale the refrigerator by holding onto the handles. Doing little things, like pushing in chairs all the way or putting stools atop counters when they're not in use will help. You will also want to always push drawers in all the way because if you don't, your toddler will climb them like stairs and get to places she shouldn't.

Part of your toddler's newfound ability to explore the air up there means that things you previously thought were out of reach no longer will be. You will need to put any potentially dangerous items where she absolutely can't get to them, preferably behind a cabinet lock. Fail to do this and leave, say, a bottle of cleaning spray on a seemingly unscalable counter, and you may stumble upon your kid (six feet off the ground) spraying it into her face. You then will have to frantically call poison control before holding your screaming toddler in the sink for twenty minutes in order to flush out her eyes. Or so the authors have been told—this certainly didn't happen to their real-life toddler. (Ahem.) This scenario, as you imagine, is best avoided.

Most importantly, you must never lower your guard and think, "I'm sure she's fine" or "There's no way she could ever do that." Instead, you must live under the assumption that your toddler is constantly conspiring to do something that could do some serious damage. More than likely, she will be.

COMMUNICATING
WITH YOUR
TODDLER

CHAPTER 2

When you first became a parent you undoubtedly peered into your newborn's tiny face and fantasized about the conversations you would have one day. You imagined giving him advice, baring your souls to each other, and laughing so hard that you'd suddenly wonder, "Did I just become best friends with my kid?" While those conversations may happen eventually (emphasis on *may*), you can be sure that nothing even remotely like this will happen during the toddler years.

To survive communicating with your toddler you will need to be incredibly patient and draw upon all of your interpretive skills. Prior experience dealing with irrational people is also very helpful. Have you ever had to chaperone a drunk friend who wanted to go to another bar even though they'd already thrown up on themselves? Or waited on a customer who pitched a fit because their burger didn't magically arrive within sixty seconds of ordering it? If so, you will be well suited for communicating with your toddler. Ready to join the conversation? Good. Let's talk it out.

EARLY TODDLER

During this stage you will be anxious for your toddler to start talking, but he probably won't be as motivated as you'd like. This is because (in far too many circumstances) he will have no need for language. When he wants some of your yogurt, he will take it (with his fingers), and when he wants your smartphone, he will swipe it. As his parent, it's your job to stop him from acting like a feral creature and to force him to actually communicate his wants and needs. This he will do through a new toddler's primary forms of communication: screaming, crying, and throwing full-blown tantrums.

When toddlers communicate this way it's easy to get frustrated, but keeping your cool and trying to understand their kicking and screaming can make the difference between suffering through or avoiding a forty-five-minute tantrum that ends with you crying too. One way you can do this is by playing a game of "Hot and Cold." Does your toddler's wailing abate ever so slightly when you move toward the refrigerator? If so, he might be hungry. To test this further, move away from the fridge. If your toddler kicks his feet even harder, you can be sure that's his way of saying, "Colder! COLDER!"

As you've likely surmised, much of what you will do to help your toddler learn to communicate will make you feel more than a little silly. For example, it's widely recommended that you narrate the things you do in front of your toddler. This means you will often find yourself alone with your toddler and saying things like, "Now I'm putting the socks in the drawer! Yes, I am! Right next to the underwear! Can you say 'underwear'?" The fact that your toddler will probably just stare back at you with a blank expression after you say this will do little to make you feel any less silly. Narrating your actions in public, however, is where you will feel the most silly, especially if you fail to make sure no one else is in the vicinity when you do it. The last thing you want is to say, "Now I'm putting a bag of rice in the cart! Rice is yummy, isn't it?" only to have an until-then-unnoticed old woman respond, "Uh, sure, dear. Rice is yummy."

Another popular way to encourage your toddler's early communication skills is by teaching him how to sign simple commands like "more," "snack," "drink," and "play." Again, you may feel a little silly signing at your toddler (especially if he only stares back at you), but it can make your lives easier if he gets the hang of it. It's recommended, though, that in addition to teaching him the aforementioned commands, you also teach him to recognize the signs for "Dude, have some chill!" and "I swear to all that is holy that if you don't stop screaming I will burn every last stuffed animal on your bed." These latter hand signs will come in especially handy when he is acting up at church, the library, or a restaurant.

Eventually your toddler will say his first word, but when he does it's important not to try to get him to repeat it

TODDLER TIP #5

Avoid talking to your toddler using "baby speak." This will not only help to improve his verbal development, it will lower your chances of getting caught saying "wee wee" or "nappy poo" in front of another adult.

in front of every person you see. The reality is that your toddler may not repeat the word again for weeks (or even months), and you will look foolish berating him to say "carrot" over and over until you finally give up and say something cringingly awkward like, "He really did say 'carrot.' I promise he did. Come on, baby. Say 'carrot.' Just once for Mama! SAY CARROT!'" Many scientists conjecture this phenomenon of toddlers gladly performing milestones in front of you (but never in front of anyone else) is intentional and their way of pranking their parents. So, if you ever see your toddler laughing with another toddler, it's most likely at your expense.

PEAK TODDLER

It will be hard to believe, but at this stage your toddler (the very same one you harassed over and over to say "carrot" in front of your mother-in-law) will now speak almost constantly and in front of everyone. The rub, though, is that his speech will be all but incomprehensible to anyone but you. As a result, you will basically become his interpreter and spend your days explaining to everyone you meet that "huffo" means "hello," "eeeeeeeese" means "cheese," and "teepee" means "TV." And since you alone can understand him, it will mean that on the rare occasion you have a kid-free night out, you will be forced to run out of the movie theater to field a call from the babysitter because your toddler is frantically shrieking "Air!" and he doesn't know why. You, of course, will know that "air" means "bear," as in

TODDLER TIP #6

If your toddler is talking too much somewhere he shouldn't (like the library), ask him what he likes about vegetables. This will render him mute within seconds.

the stuffed one your kid absolutely must have on one or two random days each month.

Calls like that from the babysitter won't be fun, but they're just the tip of the iceberg when it comes to the awkward situations your toddler's less-than-stellar pronunciation will get you into. More than anything else, you must be prepared to quickly jump in and clarify any words and phrases your toddler will say that sound inflammatory but actually aren't. For example, words like "truck" or "fork" may be innocent, but they can sound especially profane coming out of your toddler's mouth. Many a parent has seen their personal relationships damaged and suffered public humiliation because they didn't realize their toddler's pleas for a fork sounded like a flurry of F-bombs to everyone else.

The good news is that in certain circumstances your toddler's incomprehensible speech can be used to your advantage. A good example of this is when your toddler inevitably makes a wildly inappropriate comment to someone in public:

Your toddler said: *"Why is that man so fat?"*
The man: *"Excuse me?!"*
You: *"He said he . . . likes your hat."*
The man: *"Oh! Thank you!"*

Alternatively, if your toddler says something *really* inappropriate, you can feign ignorance and simply say, "That just sounded like a bunch of gibberish to me."

Ironically, while your toddler will speak almost incomprehensibly 99 percent of the time, he can suddenly become incredibly eloquent when it suits him. So, while he might sound like a drunken Bob Dylan when you ask him where his shoes are, he will speak with the crisp clarity of Sir Anthony Hopkins when he wants a treat. ("Excuse me, Mother, but could you take me out for ice cream, perchance?") You can call your toddler out on this if you choose, but be warned: parents who do so report seeing a dramatic increase in how often their toddler says things like "truck" and "fork" in front of elderly grandparents and religious leaders. This is highly unlikely to be a coincidence.

LATE TODDLER

In the late stages of toddlerhood your child will at last be able to speak clearly. This will be a welcome change at first, but only until you realize your toddler is using this newfound ability to embarrass you as often as he possibly can. Whether he does this innocently or through deliberate action (recent studies ominously suggest the latter), you must remain vigilant.

The ways your suddenly intelligible toddler can embarrass you are many and varied. If you have a touch of diarrhea in the morning, he will likely spend the rest of the day telling everyone you come into contact with about it in great detail. If you pass a man with an eye patch, he might holler, "Look, everyone! It's a pirate!" Forget to pack a snack for him at the park, and he will loudly make a show of "starving" to everyone within earshot (never mind that he ate six pancakes at breakfast less than an hour earlier). Thankfully, there are some strategies you can employ to lessen your chances of suffering this kind of toddler-inflicted embarrassment.

First, take care not to say or do anything in front of your toddler that you wouldn't be okay with him repeating in public. This can be difficult, but it's of the utmost importance. Let one "douchebag" slip while stuck in traffic, and a few days later your toddler will be yelling "douchebag" over and over in the supermarket.

Second, you can master the art of deftly interrupting your toddler. While this may be rude, it's nonetheless one of a parent's strongest weapons against embarrassment, especially when used in conjunction with distraction:

Your toddler: *"My mommy was on the phone talking to the bank this morning when she got really mad and said—"*
You: *"Look! It's Anna and Elsa right over there!"*
Your toddler: *"What?"*
You: *"Yes, with Olaf! He's got that little cloud over his head and everything. Over there by the tree. Go check it out!"*

Lastly, in extremely high-risk situations you can give your toddler a lollipop. This will quiet him for a few minutes, but you should know that every minute of silence the lollipop gives you will be paid back later with five times as many minutes of sugar-induced toddler craziness.

Late-stage toddlers can also embarrass you by *not* talking. This most often happens immediately after you've bragged to a friend or family member about how well spoken your toddler is. When this happens you can either laugh awkwardly and change the subject, or ask your toddler about one of their interests like *My Little Pony*. Choose wisely, though, because forcing your guests to listen to a ten-minute treatise on why Pinkie Pie is the best pony may very well be an alternative worse than silence.

CONVERSATIONS WITH YOUR TODDLER

Have you ever been at a party where you got stuck talking to an excruciatingly boring guest? If so, you have a good

RECORDED TODDLER DYSFUNCTION THROUGHOUT HISTORY

On March 4, 1861, twenty-five thousand people gathered on the east front of the Capitol to watch Abraham Lincoln deliver his first inaugural address. Many of those witnesses wrote accounts of the day that have passed into historical record. One account, however, is historically significant for reasons that go beyond Lincoln:

"My wife, Matilda, and our two grown sons, Mathias and Allaster, traveled for many days by carriage to see Lincoln (our fellow Illinoisan) take possession of the highest office in the land. It was a long and uncomfortable journey, but what pride we felt in our breasts upon taking our spot! Sadly, this glorious occasion was ruined not by a Southern assassin (as many feared), but a child of two or three who began to cry ten paces to our right. As the child's shrill wails grew, Lincoln became impossible to hear no matter how much I leaned forward. The mother tried to quiet the child and succeeded to a degree, but then he began to whine, 'I'm bored,' 'I want to go home,' 'I'm hungry,' and 'I need to go to the outhouse.' He repeated these demands again and again until Lincoln finished his remarks and I realized I'd heard precious little of what he had to say. Why anyone would bring a child of that age to an event like this, I do not know."

idea of what it will be like trying to converse with your toddler. Now before you take offense, you should know this is not a knock on your toddler. Toddlers are new to talking, and can't be expected to understand the many intricacies of conversation that have taken the rest of us decades to master. With that said, toddlers *are* flat-out terrible at conversing. Unfortunately, while it's permissible to tune out a boring party guest, you can't tune out your toddler because it's your job to help him develop his speaking skills. In order to remain engaged when your toddler opens his mouth, you will need to understand the many ways he will try your patience:

He will be hard to understand. While you will understand your toddler better than anyone else, there will still be times when you have to concentrate with all your might to get even the gist of what he's saying, especially when he starts using two- and three-syllable words.

He will be a low talker. Just like Kramer's one-time girlfriend on *Seinfeld*, your toddler will often seem incapable of saying anything at a discernible volume. Never mind that when he's not low talking he will be singing, laughing, and shrieking at a volume that could break glass.

He will talk about boring things. Your toddler will love to talk about things like why green is the best color, what the dog he saw at the park looked like, and why you should let him eat ice cream. At no time will he ever dish with you about what he thinks will happen next on *your* favorite TV show or bring you juicy gossip about anyone over the age of five.

He will take seemingly interminable pauses. If there's anything worse than listening to a treatise on why green is the best color, it's listening to that treatise being interrupted every few seconds by an extended pause.

He will abruptly change the subject. When you're finally getting into your toddler's explanation of why he doesn't want to wear clothes anymore, he will switch directions and start jawing about what happened on that day's episode of *Mickey Mouse Clubhouse*.

The good news is that there are things you can do to improve your chances of not zoning out on your toddler. One way is to pretend you're on the TV show *Survivor*, taking the "immunity challenge" to understand your toddler. As your kid babbles on and on, tell yourself, "You don't want to get

voted off the island, do you? Focus!" or "If we win, that's a million bucks! Get your head into the game!" If that doesn't work, think about how many more of these conversations you will have to have with your toddler if you don't help him to learn how to converse better. As far as incentive goes, that's a pretty strong one.

HOW *NOT* TO BE "PLAYED"

Your toddler may be younger than half the clothes in your closet, marginally intelligible, and still wearing diapers, but don't let that fool you—he will outsmart you if you're not careful.

The first thing you should know is that your toddler will learn the language of manipulation long before any other language. This means he will often try to get his way by exploiting his cuteness. He will bat his eyes, cock his head, and hug you while saying, "I wuv you" over and over. It's all too easy to zone out only to discover later that you handed over your smartphone, sixty bucks, and all of the candy you have in the house.

The most common method of manipulation your toddler will use will involve throwing a tantrum. Alarmingly, toddlers seem to know to do this when they have the most leverage . . . in public. When your toddler is kicking and screaming "Candy!" in front of dozens of people, it's tempting to just give him the candy, but that is a solution that will come back to bite you later because once he learns this method works he will use it again and again.

Instead of giving in, teach him that tantrums don't work by removing him from the area. Want to *really* teach him not to throw tantrums in public? Try returning to your car, strapping him into his car seat, and then slowly eating the candy he wanted. Most parents won't have enough ice water in their veins to do this, but it will seem more and more reasonable the longer you fight these toddler wars.

It's also important to understand that no matter how obvious it may be that your toddler has done wrong, he will always plead total innocence. You could find him face down in a giant chocolate cake and he will deny so much as going near it. Because of this, you should generally be skeptical of everything he says. Maintaining a healthy dose of skepticism is smart even when your toddler isn't actively trying to pull one over on you. Toddlers have trouble separating fantasy from reality, and are apt to wake you from a nap by saying, "There's a man in the backyard!" If you're not skeptical you might flip out and call the police, which could lead to you having to utter: "I'm so sorry, officer. My toddler now says he saw, uh, Spiderman."

FEEDING
YOUR TODDLER

CHAPTER 3

By the time you reach adulthood, eating has likely become one of the great, uncomplicated joys of your life. You've developed a palate for a variety of foods, including vegetables (and not just onion rings). You probably still enjoy sweets, but can stop eating them before they make you sick. And surely you can eat a meal without staining your clothes so badly they have to be thrown out. Yup, things are pretty good for you when it comes to food.

Toddlers, on the other hand, have a very complicated relationship with food. In fact, toddlers are pretty much all drama, all the time when it comes to eating. This means that as the parent of a toddler, your life will be all drama, all the time as well. So, unless you want to get fed up with getting your toddler fed, let's strategize. Bon appétit!

EMBRACING THE MESS

Embracing the messy eating habits of your toddler might be one of the hardest challenges you'll face as a parent. While you don't have to like it, you do have to accept that it's part of the learning process. Toddlers lack the coordination and attention required to keep from looking like they got into a fight with their food and lost, but they do get there eventually.

In the meantime, you have to be ready for the mess. There will be mashed potatoes dropped onto the floor, chicken nuggets hurled across the room, and napkins on spaghetti night that look they were used to clean up a crime scene. Most disturbingly, food will end up in places you never imagined food could go, like the inside of your toddler's nose, ears, and diapers. If you prepare yourself for this (and worse), it will be slightly easier to handle.

Then there's your home, which won't be the same until the toddler years are over, so you might not want to invest in any fine furnishings or decor until you've emerged on the other side. Until then, make the most of the destruction. Peanut butter handprints on the wall that won't wash off become custom artwork. A trail of Cheerios through the home might one day lead rescuers to your exhausted body.

Put an old T-shirt over your toddler to keep her from dirtying her clothes at mealtime. It's like a full-body bib!

Are these ideas extreme? Of course! But going with the flow sure beats making yourself so crazy that you end up rocking in the corner. Keeping a shred of your sanity intact is key for your survival.

It's also important to understand that teaching your toddler proper eating habits can often lead to greater messes. Using utensils, for example, is a shockingly hard skill for some toddlers to grasp, and there won't be many meals where your toddler's fork doesn't end up on the floor at least five times. In uncoordinated hands, spoons will dribble soup and cereal onto tables and clothes. Make sure you have lots of stain remover close by.

Above all, don't overemphasize neatness. Yes, you want your toddler to be clean, but you don't want to give her a complex about it. Make sure she's eating healthy stuff and take deep breaths. The laundry is just collateral damage.

MEALTIME MISSTEPS

With every meal there are tactical mistakes that can doom you from the start. Make sure you avoid the following:

- Don't become your toddler's short order cook. The first time you make her a different meal than the rest of the family won't be the last.
- Don't unload the groceries in front of her unless you want to hear immediate complaints and/or demands to eat items immediately.

- Just like you don't negotiate with terrorists, you don't negotiate with toddlers. Once you start saying, "One bite of carrots and you can have a cookie," your toddler has won. The next thing you know, a few months will pass and the rate of business will have slowly bumped up to the point where you're trading five cookies and a scoop of ice cream for that same, teensy-weensy bite of carrots.

- Don't overfill her plate. Toddlers have small stomachs and can often be overwhelmed by large amounts of food.

- Don't act like the drill sergeant from *Full Metal Jacket* and stand over your toddler screaming, "You will eat that vegetable, young lady, or so help me!" That pressure doesn't help and will only make her resent vegetables (and you).

- Don't overdo it on the fruit snacks. They're loaded with sugar and all too easy to hand out, especially when your toddler keeps running up to you every five minutes asking for you to open a new one. Instead, keep your kid hungry so that at dinner she'll actually eat instead of pushing away her dinner because her tummy is filled with 101 fruit snacks.

- Don't forget that it's a long process. Your toddler probably won't be pitching a fit and refusing veggies at twenty. If she's eating, that's a step in the right direction. Keep pushing for incremental gains.

TODDLER VISION

HOW YOU SEE THE WORLD:

HOW YOUR TODDLER SEES THE WORLD:

CANDY

If you've ever seen a horror film where zombies relentlessly come after human flesh with single-minded determination, then you've got a pretty good idea of how toddlers feel about candy. This wouldn't be a problem if candy was good for your toddler, but it's not only bad for her, it will throw your lives into disarray for hours after she's ingested it.

There are three stages your toddler will pass through after she's greedily stuffed her face with candy. In the first, she will be manically hyper for anywhere from fifteen minutes to a couple of hours, and spend that time leaping off things without any regard for her safety. In the next stage, she will be overtired and cranky, either breaking into tears for no apparent reason or throwing punches at you whenever you come within a three-foot radius of her. Finally, she will crash and nap for way longer than you like, ruining bedtime and your night.

That miserable cycle is reason enough to permanently ban candy from your toddler's life, but it's not the only reason you should. As they say on infomercials, "But wait . . . there's more!" Toddlers are also incapable of enjoying candy without making a mess, and their hands and face will be coated with chocolate even before the wrapper hits the floor. Once that happens you will have only a few seconds to jump in and clean your toddler before she wipes the chocolate onto her clothes, but be warned: if you don't deftly grab her wrists and hold them in the air as you bust out the wipes, your clothes will likely end up horribly stained too.

TODDLER TIP #8

To distract your toddler from the candy display when checking out at the supermarket, ask her to help you put items on the conveyor belt. If it's still not your turn, put items back into the cart and repeat the process.

Clearly, limiting your toddler's candy intake should be a major priority. The good news is that this is fairly easy to do in your own home—just don't bring the sweet stuff through your front door. The bad news is that, while you can control candy in your home, it becomes much harder to do once you step outside. That's because, until you have a toddler, you never realize just how *much* candy there is in public. Basically, candy is everywhere, and toddlers have a hawk-like ability to spot even two lone M&Ms from a thousand feet away.

In order to at least attempt to stay one step ahead of your toddler, you will need to immediately scan every room you enter for candy. Upon finding some, either remove it or your toddler as quickly as possible. You will also need to learn which of the aisles at the supermarket are stocked up the wazoo with candy, and have a game plan for what to do when you get into the checkout line with its impossibly large candy display. (Whoever came up with the idea of putting candy at the checkout, by the way, has a special place in hell waiting for them.)

Another major struggle you will face will be dealing with the many people in public who offer your toddler candy without consulting you first. Whenever this happens (and it will happen a lot), you will be put in the unenviable position

A RANKING OF THE BEST PLACES TO HIDE CANDY
(FROM WORST TO BEST):

5   **The highest cupboard in the kitchen:** This is a good spot until your toddler gets wind of it. After that she'll spend her free time stacking chairs to try to climb up to it, giving you more than a few gray hairs in the process.

4   **The lowest cupboard in the kitchen:** The upside here is that if your toddler figures out your hiding space there's no chance she'll fall from a great height. The downside is that she'll eat every last candy in the bag and spend the next forty-eight hours running in a circle.

3   **In the washing machine:** You will brag to all of your friends about having found the perfect hiding place until you forget your candy is in there and turn a load of whites Hershey's brown.

2   **In the vegetable drawer:** While the odds of your toddler looking in here are low, the odds of you adding more and more candy until it transforms into the "candy drawer" are high.

1   **A locked safe:** This location all but guarantees your candy will remain safely out of your toddler's hands. Just make sure your combination isn't "0000" or you might stumble upon a "master thief."

of having to either say "no," and send your toddler into a tantrum, or say "yes," and be forced to deal with the fallout for the rest of the day.

The one saving grace of candy is that (like most things of great power) it can be harnessed for good instead of evil. While using candy as a bribe to get what you want was briefly covered in the previous chapter, it will be discussed in much greater detail in the chapters to come.

VEGETABLES

Toddlers may be willing to do just about anything to eat candy, but when it comes to vegetables, the opposite is true. In fact, if it were up to them, they would subsist exclusively on mac and cheese, pizza, quesadillas, and chicken fingers, and consider a scoop of strawberry ice cream to be health food. So how can you get your toddler to eat vegetables? While it isn't easy, there are things you can do to improve your odds of eventually seeing your kid eat a vegetable without a knock-down, drag-out fight.

Have you ever been in public and spied a toddler happily chomping on a tomato or cucumber? If you have, you'd be forgiven for assuming they were a robot instead of an actual living, breathing toddler. These tots are human though (probably), and if you ask their parents what their secret is they'll generally point to two things. The first is that they introduced vegetables to their toddlers when they were still babies. This might not be possible with your kid, especially if she's already developed a taste for nacho cheese and

ketchup, but the sooner you introduce vegetables into the mix, the better the chances are that she will eat them.

The second thing these overachieving parents do is set a good example by regularly eating and enjoying vegetables themselves. If vegetables aren't a regular part of your diet, you can help the situation by making an effort to eat them, even if at first you sound like a hostage reading a prepared statement: "This vegetable is both nutritious and delicious. I am going to put it in my mouth and swallow without any difficulty, because its taste brings pleasure to me. Hooray for vegetables. Hooray." Whether you choose to do this or not is entirely up to you, but you should know that if you make a gag face when you find a stray fried zucchini in your basket of cheese fries, your toddler probably isn't going to be gorging on veggies anytime soon.

You can also encourage your toddler to eat her vegetables by saying things like, "If you eat spinach you'll get strong

TODDLER TIP #9

Toddlers love color, so try putting together a plate featuring colorful vegetables like carrots, bell peppers, broccoli, and squash. Plus ranch dressing—lots and lots of ranch dressing.

like Popeye," and "If you eat carrots you'll see better at night!" Neither of these things is actually true, of course (not even the one about carrots—that's British propaganda from World War II), so why not go one step further and tell your toddler something that will *really* make her want to eat her veggies? You could ask her if she knows that veggies will give her magical powers! Just be sure to cover your lie by telling your toddler the magic won't kick in until she's twelve or so, and only if she keeps eating her veggies. The one downside of this strategy is that people might find your kid a little (or shall we say *a lot*) strange for thinking that eating asparagus is going to turn her into Harry Potter. But so what? It's a small price to pay to have a kid who doesn't shriek in horror at the sight of a plate of vegetables.

Lastly, if your toddler absolutely refuses to eat vegetables no matter what you do, you can use a blender to "hide" them in foods she will eat like pancakes or smoothies. While this will get the vegetables' nutrients into your toddler, it won't help her overcome her aversion to veggies because she won't know she's eating them. And, making matters worse, if she ever finds out what you're doing it will make her forever suspicious of you, and lead to frustrating conversations like this:

Your kid: *"Did you put veggies in this?!"*
You: *"It's a Snickers bar."*

RECORDED TODDLER DYSFUNCTION THROUGHOUT HISTORY

Japan's greatest master of the haiku, Matsuo Bashō, was born in 1644 to a samurai, but turned his back on the military to live the life of a poet. He found much of his inspiration by wandering the country, and on one of these journeys was given shelter by a young family. While there he composed haikus about the family's picky-eating two-year-old. The poems, while firmly ranked among his lesser works, shed fascinating light on the historical toddler:

> "He begs her for rice
> But once it is made and served
> He now wants noodles"

> "One vegetable
> Is all that his mother asks
> But plated it stays"

> "Child screams and hollers
> Mother screams and hollers back
> Father eats his food"

> "Child cries in anger
> Eggplant is touching his fish
> A crime, it would seem"

> "Under the table
> Child drops fresh fish, rice, and bowl
> What a freaking brat"

Your kid: *"Answer the question."*
You: *"It's still in its wrapper."*
Your kid: *"JUST ANSWER THE QUESTION!"*

To avoid having this happen to you, it's best to purée the vegetables when your toddler is out of the house, preferably no less than five to ten miles away.

PROTECTING YOUR FOOD

If there's one type of food that toddlers will always want to eat without reservation, it's *your* food. This means that in order to continue enjoying your meals and snacks, your usual three-step routine of going to the kitchen, preparing food, and then eating it will now have a new wrinkle: using ninja-like subterfuge.

Thankfully, there is a trick that works well during the early stages of toddlerhood. When you've made yourself a bowl of, say, spinach and artichoke dip, and your toddler comes running for it while shouting "Mine!", quickly point to the bowl and say, "Spicy!" This will likely stop her in her tracks, as will saying other words you know she'll respond poorly to, such as "Hot!" or "Pickles!" Just don't make the mistake some parents have made, which is to tell their toddler that their food is gross because it's made of poop. This could lead to an embarrassing situation in public where your toddler desperately reaches for your food and screams, "PLEASE! I WANT YOUR POOP! LET ME EAT YOUR POOP!"

If you're having trouble finding your toddler, loudly make some food in the kitchen. This will make her come running as if by Pavlovian response.

Unfortunately, as your toddler ages this trick will become less effective. To up the ante, try plopping a jalapeño onto whatever you're eating. You can even do this with ice cream and tell your toddler, "Why yes, son, I am eating ice cream! It's jalapeño-flavored and very spicy! Sorry, pal!" If you're out of jalapeños or simply don't want even one near your food, parsley can also make a very effective toddler repellent. Just be sure that when you use this trick successfully you don't let a "Mwahahahahaha" escape from your lips. When you have a toddler, you must keep all maniacal laughs on the inside.

Eventually, none of these tricks will thwart your toddler, and you will need to take other measures. One is to establish a firm "no toddlers on your lap" rule while eating, because once your toddler has weaseled her way onto your lap and put herself between you and your food, she's won. Your food might as well be her food.

Another measure you can take is to make more food than you can eat, knowing that your toddler will want some of it. Do not, however, make the mistake of preparing your toddler a plate of this food ahead of time—*that* food she won't want (even if it did come out of the same pot as yours). Instead, wait for you toddler to beg for what's on your plate, then scoop the surplus you accounted for onto a plate for her.

Finally, no discussion of how to safeguard food from your toddler would be complete without covering how you can enjoy sugary treats without having them ripped from your hands. The best way to do this is by waiting until late at night when your toddler is deep in REM sleep, but many parents can't wait that long. If you fall into this category, you must be sure never to eat anything sweet within the general vicinity of your toddler. Often parents will covertly toss a chocolate into their mouth, then (thinking they're in the clear) return to their toddler's side while still chewing. This is a serious tactical error, though, because toddlers can tell the difference between when you're chewing something boring and chewing something delicious. You will then be stuck listening to cries of "Want candy!" for the next hour or until you give in and share your stash.

A more effective way to sneak a daytime treat is by absconding to the bathroom. This method is not without its drawbacks, though. First, it means leaving your toddler alone for the thirty to sixty seconds it will take you to frantically cram a candy bar into your mouth, and that's more than enough time for her to wreak havoc on your home. Second, even if your toddler doesn't sense a disturbance in the force and come running, you're still stuck eating your treat in the bathroom. Hard as it may be to wait, night is the best time to enjoy your sugary fix—just be sure to listen for the sound of toddler feet hurriedly padding your way.

EATING AWAY FROM THE TABLE

If you think toddlers are messy when they're sitting down to eat at the table, they are downright slovenly when you're on the go. It's as if they lose all sense of where their mouth is without a table in front of them.

At home, your toddler *will* want snacks away from the table. You'll be tempted to give her simple ones like popcorn in front of the TV or chips while she plays with toys. Those snacks may seem innocent enough, but it's still best to have a firm rule about not eating away from the table. Why? Because once you give your toddler an inch she will take a mile. She will slowly ask for food that is more complicated (and messy) until one day you're finding a slice of pizza in the bathroom, pudding inside of shoes, and moldy string cheese in your toddler's bed. Clearly, it's best to keep your toddler seated for all eating at home to avoid this trajectory.

There is an important exception. In the car, your toddler will demand snacks the second you leave for your destination. While you can try to have a "no eating" rule there, too, this often leads to a hungry toddler, which is the worst kind of toddler there is, especially on the road. Because of this, many parents decide that enjoying (relative) peace and quiet in the car is worth having smashed fish crackers on the floor and half-chewed gummies stuck to the seats. To help limit messes (and to make things as easy on you as possible) buy single-serving snacks or create your own with baggies before you leave the house. Why single-serving sizes? Because if you hand your toddler a full-size bag of pretzels, you can bet it will be overturned onto the floor within thirty seconds of the handoff, making a mess and making your toddler cry.

There are many other locations you will need to feed your toddler, each of which comes with its own challenges. At the beach, for example, you should never pack anything overly sticky or your toddler will cry for hours about sand being stuck to her food. Playgrounds will make your kids filthy, so consider bringing along food that can be eaten with utensils. And if you try something absolutely crazy—like going to a museum—only bring along food that can be quickly shoved into your toddler's mouth inside a bathroom stall. Also, never, ever forget a drink. If you do, you'll be forced to listen to whiny cries of "I'm thirsty!" until you somehow track down a beverage.

Lastly, you should always try to avoid the most dangerous "away from the table" food: ice cream. Often it will pop up suddenly in the form of an ice cream truck or pushcart. If there aren't other kids around, you can usually distract your toddler from noticing the moving freezers, but once she does, the jig is up. When that happens you should make your toddler sit down to eat her treat, but you'll still need to be prepared for the ice cream to run down her arms onto her shirt, pants, and feet. And you'll need plenty of wipes—forget them, and your kid will wipe her sticky fingers off in her hair.

 TODDLER TIP #11 Always have an emergency snack (such as gummies) stashed away in your purse or car. You never know when you might be stuck in a line and your toddler will find herself dying of hunger. Just resist the urge to eat it yourself.

GROOMING YOUR TODDLER

CHAPTER 4

From a distance, toddlers can look like nothing short of the cutest little things in the world, but up close they're liable to make your stomach turn. That's because they spend their days covering themselves in boogers, dirt, sand, chocolate stains, pizza sauce, crushed ants, dried ice cream, mom's makeup, dad's shaving cream, melted cheese, allegedly washable kid's glue, Play-Doh, and about a thousand other things. As the parent of a toddler, your unenviable task is to keep your whirlwind from looking like a living and breathing version of Pigpen from *Peanuts*.

The task is even harder than it seems, because toddlers don't want to be clean either. They will fight you every step of the way on the road toward cleanliness, and they aren't afraid to fight dirty to stay dirty. So grab your soap, washcloth, and wipes. It's time to learn the things you need to know so that your toddler doesn't become "*that* kid."

BRUSHING UP

In their darkest hours, many frustrated parents of toddlers think, "Why do I torture myself trying to brush this kid's teeth? They're just baby teeth! In a few years the permanent ones will come in and then we can start brushing—when my kid is more reasonable!" While this line of thinking is alluring, you mustn't let yourself be seduced by it. Teaching your toddler good oral care is important, and toddler breath can be stinky (so the brushing is as much for you as it is for your kid). Unfortunately, while you do have to clean your toddler's teeth, it isn't easy. Your toddler will do everything he can to resist until he breaks you and wins the right to go to bed with fishies and fruit snacks stuck between his teeth.

Your first challenge will be to get the toothbrush into your toddler's mouth. While many dentists suggest you "pleasantly persuade" your toddler to open his mouth, you will likely find "pleasant persuasion" ineffective as your toddler clenches his teeth and flails about. Instead, try tickling your toddler. When he laughs, you will have a clear path into his mouth.

Once you get the toothbrush into your toddler's mouth you must be prepared for him to bite down on it over and over. He will also reach up and try to swat your hand away, so you may have to pin his hands down. Because this is very stressful, it is easy to unknowingly shorten your toddler's brushing sessions over time from a solid couple of minutes to about seven seconds. To avoid having this happen to you, try setting a timer when you start.

It should be mentioned that there is some anecdotal evidence that you can make the experience less miserable by distracting your toddler while brushing. This is worth trying by singing a silly made-up song ("Crazy Mr. Tooth Wants to Get Clean!"), showing him a video (one of himself is best, since toddlers are little narcissists), or letting him play with your phone (just make sure he isn't so close to the toilet that he can drop it into the water).

Some parents suggest allowing your toddler to brush his own teeth, but this will likely end with him sucking off all of the toothpaste before listlessly holding the brush in his mouth. Others will advise you to buy your toddler a toothbrush with a theme based on his favorite TV show or movie; however, you should know that your toddler will likely just play with it instead of actually brushing.

Last, but not least, you need to be prepared for your toddler's first visit to the dentist. While these are actually fairly easy trips because they have plenty of kids' movies and toys on hand, the dentist will ask you if you've been flossing your toddler's teeth. It is important to know this now so you can respond with a convincing "yes" instead of laughing out loud.

HANDS AND NAILS

More often than not, your toddler's hands will look like a mechanic's at the end of a twelve-hour shift. Amazingly, this can even be true twenty minutes after he's woken up and ventured no further than the family room. How your toddler manages to do this is a mystery, but your job as his parent is not. You must keep his hands as clean as possible, not only to lower his chances of getting sick, but to avoid receiving judgy looks in public for toting around a toddler with seemingly radioactive hands.

First and foremost, you need to understand that cleaning a toddler's hands is not for the faint of heart. You're guaranteed to come into contact with all kinds of sticky, stomach-turning substances, and what you'll find under his nails will be even worse: remnants of yesterday's lunch, dirt, dark stuff you *hope* is dirt, boogers, and a whole lot of other unwanted surprises. Because of this (and because you will be cleaning his hands and nails regularly) it is imperative that you learn to keep down your lunch.

While there is no great secret to cleaning a toddler's hands besides using lots of soap, you will need to make sure the water is the right temperature. If it's too hot or too cold, your toddler will yank his hands out from under the water,

continued on page 72

"THE BANKER"

This toddler picks up every single coin he comes across including ones found in the gutter. Consequently, his hands are covered in grime and his entire body reeks of copper.

"THE TATTOO ARTIST"

This toddler must be kept away from pens and markers because she sees her entire body as her canvas. Given the chance she will cover every inch of skin with modern art-esque doodles and her face with markings even Mike Tyson would describe as "a bit much."

"THE CHEF"

This toddler doesn't just eat food, he experiences it. Leave him unsupervised in the kitchen for even a minute and he will quickly cover himself in ketchup, mayo, orange juice, and lunch meat.

"THE DESSERT LOVER"

This toddler is similar to The Chef but will be on the lookout for sweets and sweets only. It doesn't matter if the sweets are out of sight, she will find them. As a result, the area around her mouth is always stained with chocolate and her hands are sticky yet marvelous smelling.

"THE PLUMBER"

This toddler sees the bathroom as his playroom and goes there every chance he gets to endlessly flush the toilet and crawl around the toilet bowl. He loves to touch everything in a public bathroom, too, and smells like it.

"THE MAKEUP ARTIST"

This toddler is always scheming to get into her mother's makeup bag, and can cover her entire body with lipstick, foundation, and mascara before her mother realizes things suddenly got "too quiet."

"THE ZOOLOGIST"

This toddler loves holding lizards, frogs, roly-polies, worms, and other creepy crawlers nearly as much as he loves petting every dog, cat, and rodent he comes across. He usually has cobwebs in his hair and smells like nature (but not in a good way).

"THE GARDENER"

This toddler spends every minute she can outside on her hands and knees exploring the soil. She always has dirt under her fingers and smeared on her face, and a dozen ants or more crawling on her body, usually unbeknownst to her.

TODDLER TIP #12

An easy (and very effective) way to clean under your toddler's nails is with a nailbrush, warm water, and lots of soap.

then kick and scream until he escapes your grasp and runs as far away from the sink as he possibly can. As if that weren't bad enough, from that day forward he will distrust your water temperature-setting skills and shout "No! No! No!" every time you try to wash his hands. To avoid having this happen you will need to learn how to mix the hot and cold faucets with the precision of a chemist.

The hand washing problems you will face at home, however, will pale in comparison to the ones you'll deal with in public bathrooms. There, you must perform a juggling act as you lift your toddler up to the sink with one hand while turning on the water and forcing his hands under it with the other. And if the faucet is the kind that you have to continue holding down in order to make the water come out . . . good luck! Once (or, IF) you complete that, you will then need to dry your toddler's hands. This is generally easy, unless the bathroom only has a hand blower. In those godless bathrooms your toddler will shrink away from the hand blower, wailing in fear. If you find yourself in this situation, it is generally best to let him wipe his hands on your pants—vanity be damned.

BATH TIME

Toddlers either love or hate baths, which means you need to be prepared for yours to scream bloody murder going in (if he hates it) or coming out (if he loves it). Love it or hate it, though, your toddler will bring the drama with him at bath time.

If your toddler hates the tub, you can try to improve the situation by getting to the bottom of why he hates it. Of course, some toddlers simply hate getting clean and prefer to remain in their natural state of filth. There isn't much you can do for those toddlers, but others have a specific reason why they don't like to bathe. For example, some are afraid

TODDLER TIP #13

Put a laundry basket into the tub for your toddler to sit in—it will keep his bath toys from floating out of reach.

they might be sucked down the drain. If your toddler shares this fear, it might be helpful to explain (and demonstrate) how it is literally impossible for this to happen. Just be prepared for him not to believe you because toddlers aren't big on reason.

A far more common thing toddlers hate is having to wash their hair. Your toddler will likely try to convince you to skip this part of the bath (as if his hair isn't full of playground sand and curdled milk clumps) but you mustn't let yourself be swayed. Take heed, though: your toddler might stand up when you dump water on his head, so make sure you have a firm grip on one of his arms to save you from having a mini heart attack.

One of the best ways to keep your toddler busy in the bath (and thus not wreaking havoc) is to fill the tub with lots of bath toys. It is important to remember, however, that bath toys are toys, and if you misplace your toddler's favorite one at bath time, all hell will break loose.

Speaking of all hell breaking loose, or more specifically poop breaking loose, toddlers are known to poop during baths. If your toddler does this, you will need to immediately get him out of the tub, locate the offending item (a real challenge if you were giving him a bubble bath), dispose of it, then drain and clean the tub. And if any bath toys ended up, shall we say, in the line of fire, you will need to wash them too (especially dolls with hair). Blech.

Considering all of this, you must be careful that you don't fall prey to "bath denial." Bath denial is when you and your exhausted partner convince yourselves your hopelessly dirty toddler is actually clean enough to skip yet another bath. How will you know when you are suffering from bath denial? You will start having conversations like this:

"He doesn't need a bath, does he?"
"Nah. He looks fine to me."
"Agreed. I mean, we just gave him a bath. When was it?
Last Thursday?"
"Monday, actually. But he smells fine if you don't get too close."
"Absolutely. Clean as a whistle."

HAIR CARE

Care for a toddler's hair long enough and you will start to wonder why you don't see more toddlers sporting shiny domes like The Rock. Still, with a healthy dose of patience you can make it to the other side of toddlerhood without resorting to busting out the balding clippers.

In addition to the previously discussed hair washing struggles, you will find combing your toddler's hair to be a major challenge. Your toddler will not only recoil at the mere sight of a brush, but scream, "Ow!" before you've even combed a single strand of his hair. This will infuriate you. Your anger will only grow when you make the gentlest of strokes and he cries out, but it is important not to shout, "I'm barely doing anything!" If you remain relaxed, your

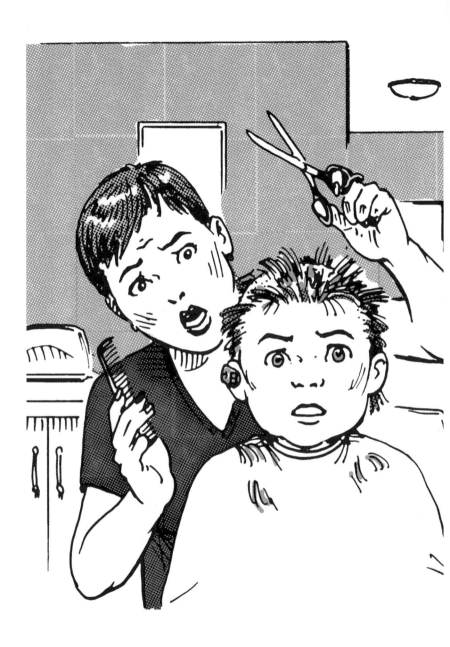

CHAPTER 4

toddler will likely stop short of becoming totally hysterical, and you should be able to shape his hair into something other than a bird's nest and get out the door.

A major key to remaining patient is lowering your expectations. Those incredible toddler hairstyles you see on Pinterest with the epic braids or perfect faux hawk? Do. Not. Attempt. Going down that road will only lead to lots and lots of tears . . . and your toddler will likely be crying too. Instead, use simple hairstyles you won't be devastated to see ruined five minutes after you walk out the door (which is about as long as most toddler hairstyles last).

When it comes time for your toddler to get a haircut (not a head shave but an actual haircut), it is best to go to a kid's hair salon. Those places may cost a bit more, but a toddler's first few haircuts tend to be screaming, crying, and flailing affairs, and subjecting a hair dresser at a regular salon to that is tantamount to cruel and unusual punishment. Your toddler's hair will look a lot better, too, thanks to a hair dresser who is used to giving these kinds of haircuts and the sedating effects of the salon's toys, iPads, and lollipops.

Finally—and this should go without saying—you should never attempt to cut your toddler's hair. The results will be at best very, very unattractive, and at worst require a trip to the emergency room.

CLOTHING

One of the more enjoyable things about having a baby is getting to dress him in precious little outfits that make people swoon. The little lacy socks! The adorable hats! You love shopping for your baby supermodel and take tremendous pride in showing him off. That's why it's such a shock when, almost overnight, your baby becomes a toddler and puts an end to your stylist days.

Your toddler will likely exert his independence by insisting on dressing himself, which means that he will often end up leaving the house looking like a colorblind hobo. And don't even think about mentioning to him that purple plaid and orange polka dots don't go together unless you want to start an epic battle. When you fight with a toddler over clothes, no one wins.

There is the rare toddler who doesn't care about his attire, but if you end up with one of these you shouldn't get too excited about this stroke of "luck." That's because putting these toddlers into a nice outfit all but guarantees certain disaster. Either someone will hand him a giant, sticky lollipop, or he'll come across a mud puddle and suddenly lose his balance. Regardless of what type of toddler you end up with, though, you need to know that they all have an incredible knack for staining their clothes with things that are almost impossible to wash like chocolate, ketchup, or grass stains (often all on the same day). Even if you think you're safe inside the house, your toddler will inevitably find your makeup bag and use your lipstick to not only paint the walls, but his clothes too.

When you need to venture into public with your toddler, don't forget your stash of stain-fighting tools. A stain remover stick fits nicely in a purse and is a good first-line of defense against whatever disgusting thing your toddler will inevitably drop down the front of his shirt. You can even leave a bottle of Spray 'n Wash in your car for larger spills. You'll want to pack a change of clothes for your toddler too, unless you're cool with your kid walking around all day with a perfect grease imprint of a slice of pizza on his shirt.

Finally, never *ever* dress your toddler in white. Instead, try to dress him in clothes that match the food he will be eating. Going out for pizza? Put him in a red shirt! Know your kid is going to get a chocolate sundae? Dress him in brown! Playing at the park? Invest in green pants and call it a day. Your washing machine will thank you.

SOCIALIZING YOUR TODDLER

CHAPTER 5

Considering all of the chaos toddlers create, you might think it's only fair to warn people not to come within a ten-foot radius of your kid (and maybe even not to make eye contact with her). Unfortunately, while this may spare some of the people you come across from suffering serious toddler-related trauma, the reality is that your toddler needs to interact with others in order to become a fully functioning, normal member of society.

Will these interactions be awkward? You betcha. Will you need to do a lot of apologizing? Absolutely. Will you be tempted to point at your toddler and say, "I don't know her?" Almost certainly. But you simply cannot keep your toddler in a bubble and expect her to ever play well with others. Ready for your toddler to start getting social? Good. Let's look at some of the people she will almost definitely be offending, *ahem*, befriending.

BABYSITTERS

When you have a toddler (especially one who has reached peak levels of toddler craziness) the idea of leaving her alone with anyone other than a close family member will be enough to make you break into a cold sweat. Nevertheless, there will more than likely come a time when you will need to do just that. This could be so you can attend a family wedding, go to an appointment, or simply take a "My head will explode and rain down from the heavens like confetti if I have to spend another minute with my toddler" day. Whatever the reason, finding someone up to the task is imperative.

Ideally, you will be able to find a babysitter who is a parent themselves. Why? Because parents have already fought their own toddler wars, and when your toddler acts up they'll be like (spits out tobacco juice), "This ain't my first rodeo, kid. Now get in bed." With that said, you shouldn't rule out hiring a babysitter without kids or even one who is—gasp!—a teenager. In the end, the main criteria you should use to judge a babysitter, regardless of their age or background, is whether you would want them by your side during a zombie apocalypse. If you think they could keep their cool in a truly nightmarish scenario, they will probably be able to handle your toddler too.

On nights when your toddler is with a babysitter, remind yourself not to freak out (and possibly drive off the road) upon looking in your rearview mirror and seeing that your toddler's car seat is empty.

Once you find the right person, there are things you can do to make their time with your toddler as endurable as possible. First, locate everything your toddler might want while you're gone (such as favorite toys, sippy cups, and the princess pajamas she *must* wear to bed) and place them out for your babysitter. You should also be very diligent in preparing an information sheet. Will it seem like overkill when you hand your babysitter a multi-page document? Maybe at the start of the night. But two hours later, when you're unreachable and your toddler is losing her mind because she was given "the wrong fork," your babysitter will appreciate item 72B on page four, which explains that your toddler will only eat mac and cheese with her *Finding Dory* fork. Just make sure the information on the sheet is accurate. Putting stuff on there that is wishful thinking, such as a bedtime that is an hour earlier than your kid's actual bedtime, will only set your babysitter up for disaster.

When it comes time to leave, it is important to know that your toddler will try to make you feel as bad as possible. She will burst into tears and desperately reach for you while screaming, "Don't go, mama! Don't go, dada! Pwease!" Keep in mind that this psychological warfare employed by your toddler is designed to stop you from leaving her with the babysitter. But you shouldn't let it sway you into staying home or taking her with you. If you do, you might find yourself in awkward situations like this:

You: *"Sorry she cried through the vows. They were beautiful. What I could hear of them, that is."*
Bride: *"The invitation said 'no kids.'"*

You: *"I know, but she seemed really sad when we tried to leave."*
Bride: *" . . . "*

To avoid getting yourself into a mess like that, remind yourself that you are leaving your toddler with a responsible individual and not the toddler-eating troll from under the bridge. Repeating the following mantra helps too: "Everything will be okay."

Once you've hit the road, you shouldn't become the "ghost in the room." Parents who do this call and text the babysitter constantly for updates. (You: "How are things now?!" Babysitter: "You mean as opposed to three minutes ago?") Since this makes it very hard for the babysitter to develop a rapport with your toddler, you should do your best to suppress the urge to pick up your phone every five minutes and instead let the babysitter and your toddler do their thing.

GRANDPARENTS

On the surface, grandparents seem like terrific people for your toddler to interact with. After all, they love you and your toddler unconditionally. They tend to think your toddler is adorable even when she's acting more unruly than a rock star in a hotel room. And while for the most part grandparents *will* be terrific for your toddler, you'll also need to be prepared for them to seriously frustrate you.

One thing that will definitely frustrate you is the unending patience grandparents have for their grandkids.

This unending patience is generally a good thing, but it also means that they will let your toddler get away with way more than you would allow. Grandparents rarely discipline, and what's worse is that they'll do everything they can to work your toddler into a tizzy. Grandpa will sneak her some candy while grandma will give her as many freshly baked cookies as her chubby hands can hold. Don't expect your toddler to nap off all those sweets while she's with them, either. There are no rules at grandma and grandpa's house, which means that when your toddler comes home, you will have to spend the next day or two re-training her not to act like a total lunatic.

Perhaps most frustratingly, grandparents will always be on the side of your toddler. Even when you all agree your toddler did something wrong, it will never be her fault in grandma and grandpa's eyes. Common grandparent excuses (CGE) include: "She probably didn't get enough sleep last night," "She's just a baby," and "I *never* allowed *you* to act like that." However, if you try to discipline your toddler in front of your parents, they will likely react angrily . . . at *you*. This will be especially confusing because they never had a problem disciplining *you* when you were a kid.

Still, grandparents are wonderful to have in your toddler's life. The unending patience definitely comes in handy when your toddler does something way over the line, like break your mom's antique grand piano. "That's okay, dear," grandma will say. "I wasn't all that fond of that piano anyway." And if your toddler snaps your dad's thousand-dollar bamboo fishing rod? "Eh, I spend too much time fishing," he'll say. "It's for the best. In fact, I should thank our little cutie!"

Grandparents will also give your toddler the undivided attention you can't always provide because of A) your job, B) having to constantly clean up after your toddler, and C) utter exhaustion. Grandparents never seem to mind playing the same game fifteen times, repeatedly going over the same flashcards, or speaking in an Elmo voice. This is great news for your toddler's development! They'll also happily buy your toddler necessities like shoes and clothes, and tack on non-necessities like toys and giant stuffed animals in the same trip. Don't have space for a giant, four-foot-tall panda? Too bad! Your toddler pointed at it and they're sending one home with her! It lives with you now.

Lastly, always remember that when your toddler has pushed you to the brink, grandparents are there to take your toddler away so you don't pull her over with you. And as they cackle about payback and how you got a child just like yourself, keep in mind that one day you might also be a grandparent. Then you'll get your opportunity for revenge.

OTHER TODDLERS

Introducing your toddler to other toddlers seems like a fabulous idea in theory. After all, toddlers share a lot in common, like their size, lack of communication skills, and the ability to frustrate yet charm every adult around them. However, before you waste too much time day dreaming about all of adorable things your toddler will do with her little toddler friends, you should know that toddler interactions are a whole lot weirder than they are cute.

The playing rituals of toddlers can be especially weird. Toddlers will often circle each other, refusing to look in the other's direction or to even acknowledge their existence. You might be tempted to force them to interact, but if you do, it will only make them avoid each other even more. When you see your toddler acting like this you might think, "This is horrible. I've given birth to a rude little a-hole!" but the good news is your toddler isn't being rude, she simply hasn't reached the stage where she's able to connect with another child her age. Yes, it looks weird, but it's normal.

Later, when your toddler is able to play with other toddlers, you'll probably find yourself longing for the days

when she couldn't. This is because toddlers aren't exactly known for their stellar sharing skills, and there's no one in the world they want to share with less than another toddler. That action figure your toddler has barely glanced at all day? It will suddenly become her most prized possession the second her playmate touches it. Toddlers will even fight over a stick like it's made out of gold and not, in fact, wood that was recently peed on by someone's dog. When this happens, it's a good time to step in to teach your child about sharing. (It's also a good time to invest in earplugs to protect your eardrums against all the high-pitched shrieking that will inevitably ensue.)

As if that weren't bad enough, some toddlers will become physical when they're angry or frustrated. This can be especially true of toddlers with older siblings, many of whom have learned out of necessity to throw punches like a boxer. If your toddler gets into a physical altercation, you must be prepared to pick up the pieces (hopefully not literally) and encourage her to use her words instead of her fists. (Or if she doesn't have any words, her points and grunts.)

With all of that said, you should still welcome play dates because it's important for your toddler to spend time around and to learn from kids her own age. And let's be honest, it's also important for you, the parent, to be around people your age too. Find a toddler who has a parent you like and your play dates will be that much more enjoyable.

Compare battle notes, console each other, and stuff your faces with candy while the toddlers are distracted. You've earned it.

RANDOM STRANGERS

Taking a toddler into public is always a dicey proposition, and few moments are dicier than when a stranger (even a kindly one) tries to strike up a conversation with your kid. In most instances this isn't because you're worried about what the stranger will do, but because you're worried about what your incredibly unpredictable, quick-to-tantrum toddler will do.

TODDLER TIP #15

Don't immediately answer for your toddler when she's asked something. This will send the message that she doesn't have to answer and stop her from becoming comfortable talking to others.

Whenever possible, you should avoid getting into these encounters. One way to do this is by scanning your surroundings for those who are most likely to want to chat up your toddler: sweet-looking old people and overly cheerful young adults. While scanning, it's important to remember that not all old people are potential conversation starters. If you see, for example, a cantankerous old man or an old woman who liberally swings her cane at people in her way, you should feel at ease. Similarly, not all young adults should make you sweat. You can feel confident that those who are dressed like hipsters will act like your toddler doesn't exist. In both instances, it is the happy ones you must be wary of. Do you see old people who look like they might play Mr. and Mrs. Claus at the mall in the winter? Or smiling young adults who look like they've never had their hearts broken? If so, those are the ones you need to hurry past like nature is calling.

The good news is that if an interaction with a stranger becomes unavoidable your toddler will get a chance to become more comfortable talking to non-family members. Just be warned: it may be painfully awkward. Because of this, you should be very conservative in your expectations of your toddler. Do not expect her to answer a lot of questions or to give elaborate, funny, or charming answers (regardless of how verbose, funny, or charming she is at home). Instead, focus on getting her to be comfortable saying "Hi," "Thank

TEN EXCUSES TO USE WHEN YOUR TODDLER WON'T RESPOND TO A STRANGER

It's awkward when someone says, "Hi, Cutie!" "What's your name?" or "How old are you?" and your toddler only stares back blankly. Thankfully, these handy excuses can break the silence:

"Sorry, she only speaks Bulgarian."

"It's not you. She sees dead people and there's a ghost standing over your shoulder."

"She actually did say hello back, but telepathically."

"It's a tough time right now. She just found out her favorite show was taken off Netflix."

"She's holding her tongue because she has bad breath and doesn't want to offend you."

"She's practicing for a movie role. She was just cast in the next Matt Damon flick as 'Shy Toddler Number Two.'"

"She's just lost in thought. I just asked her why Daniel Tiger and his dad don't wear pants but everyone else they know does."

"I think she's scared because you're a dead ringer for the villain in her favorite TV show!"

"It's my bad. I just gave her the 'don't talk to strangers talk' and did a freaking amazing job."

"She has to pee."

you," and her name. And don't sweat it if your toddler acts shy and hides behind your leg. Pushing her to do more than she's comfortable with will only make her future encounters with Mr. and Mrs. Claus types more difficult.

On the flip side, it's also possible that your toddler will act incredibly familiar with strangers and totally overstep her bounds. She could hug the stranger, eat the stranger's food, even pull the stranger's hair! If this happens you will, of course, need to teach your toddler what is and isn't appropriate—and fast.

YOUNGER SIBLINGS

Adding to your family when you have a toddler, to paraphrase Jim Gaffigan, is kind of like being handed a baby when you're already drowning. To be fair, Gaffigan was talking about what it's like to have a fourth child when he used that analogy, but make no bones about it—parenting a toddler and a baby at the same time will regularly approach four-kid levels of stress.

We realize, of course, that avoiding this situation may not be possible for many of you, so we've decided to go ahead and discuss the strategies that can make it a little more endurable. Keep in mind, though, that no strategy beats waiting to add to your family until after your toddler grows out of the phase where she's acting like a thirty-pound version of Gary Busey in a bad mood.

Before your baby arrives, your toddler will likely be excited about the prospect of having a younger sibling. If

TODDLER TIP #16

Reading a book like *You're Getting a Baby Brother/Sister!* to your toddler before the baby arrives is important, but it's just as important to reread it once the baby arrives to help her understand what she is going through.

you're lucky, her excitement will last for days or even weeks after the baby has come home. It's even possible that she will be among the very small percentage of toddlers whose excitement lasts months! (Those good-tempered toddlers are currently being studied by toddlerologists who believe they may hold the key to finding a cure for the modern toddler.) In the end, though, just about all toddlers will grow weary of sharing the spotlight with their family's latest star, which spells bad news for you.

Jealousy, more than anything else, is what will cause your toddler to act up. She'll have gone from being the headliner to the opening act, and she won't like it. What she really won't like, though, is all of the time the baby will take from her. This means that in order to get your attention she will misbehave by throwing tantrums, breaking things, and throwing food. Toddlers, you see, definitely believe in the old adage, "There's no such thing as bad press." Most infuriatingly, she will decide she desperately needs your attention the second you start doing something for the baby. Breastfeeding? That's when your toddler will *need* you to get her a toy out of the closet she hasn't thought about for months. Changing a diaper? That's when your toddler will absolutely *need* you to watch her reenact a scene from *Wreck-It Ralph*.

You may also notice your toddler regressing after the baby has come home. While getting to watch a real-life

The Curious Case of Benjamin Button might be sort
ng for a few minutes, you will quickly grow tired
ɔur formerly upright toddler crawl around on the
floor and babble like a baby.

The fun doesn't stop there, though! Once your baby is old enough to grab your toddler's toys, there will be war. Soon your kids will each be screaming so loudly that you'll wonder if they're having a competition to see who can break glass first.

So, what can you do to cope (besides breaking down while eating raw cookie dough at two in the morning)? First, you can make your toddler feel more involved in things by finding ways to let her help care for the baby. You can ask for her advice ("Do you think we should change his diaper since it smells like the New York subway in the summer? You do? Me too.") or give her a task, like bringing over the boppy during feedings. Another way to help your toddler bond with the baby is by making her believe she alone has a special power to make the baby stop crying. Invite her over when the baby starts crying, then, when the baby calms down, tell her it was because of her. This will help her connect with the baby even if in reality she does far more to make the baby cry than to calm her.

Making an effort to spend some one-on-one time with your toddler each day is a good idea too. Even just fifteen minutes of play will go a long way toward making her feel more secure (and less likely to throw a tantrum that'll have your neighbors calling in a noise complaint).

OLDER SIBLINGS

Here's the good news: If you were forced to play a real-life version of the game "Would You Rather?" and your options were A) have a toddler and an older kid, or B) have a toddler and a baby, you can and should pick "A" every time. Older kids can be incredibly helpful in raising a toddler, but (full disclosure) they can also turbo charge a toddler's bad behavior like no one else. In fact, if you're not careful, option "A" can cause you to cry-eat cookie dough at 2:00 a.m. every bit as much as option "B."

One of the greatest benefits of having older kids is that they will make your toddler fight tooth and nail for almost everything: snacks, toys, TV shows, even your attention. This will make her scrappy and resilient, and by the time she gets to preschool she'll be ready to run the place.

Your toddler will also learn how to socialize with other kids on the rare occasion that your older kids get bored enough to play with her. These play sessions will be a boon for you, too, because you will actually be able to sit down and relax for a moment.

Another great thing about having older kids is that they will likely be within those prime tattle-telling years of five to twelve. So, whether it's "Mom! She's drinking your mommy juice!" or "Dad! She's trying to cut the dog's hair," you will have advance warning and be able to stop your toddler from getting too deep into trouble most of the time.

After reading all of that, you're probably thinking life sounds grand. But in addition to the good stuff, your older

RECORDED TODDLER DYSFUNCTION THROUGHOUT HISTORY

On August 19, 2003, ninety-three-year-old Aubrey (née Vanderbilt) Pennington passed away surrounded by her children, Chet, Todd, and Brittany. That night, Chet and Brittany found the following note among her personal documents:

"Dear Chet, Todd, and Brittany,
If you are reading this it means I have passed away, and so the time has come to reveal my most closely held secret: I was not, in fact, born with the name Aubrey Vanderbilt. I was born Shoshana Moskovitz to Ukrainian immigrants in Brooklyn, and through them—in August of 1931—I was able to take a position as sitter to a toddler named Milli. Upon beginning my first day I was shocked to learn that Milli's father was none other than Benjamin "Bugsy" Siegel! Mr. Siegel gave me one order and one order only—to keep Milli quiet as he met with his associates. I thought this would be easy, but to my horror Milli was a nightmare. If I couldn't find her blanket, she would scream. If I didn't know the words to the song she requested, she would wail. And if I refused to give her candy, she would shriek! Sweat poured off my forehead as Mr. Siegel barreled into the room and sternly warned me that if I knew what was good for me I would shut Milli up. When he left, his cook sheepishly told me I was Milli's seventh babysitter. When I asked what happened to sitters one through six, he said they wore cement shoes at the bottom of the Hudson. I immediately dumped the tantruming toddler into the cook's arms and fled not just Mr. Siegel's home, but the city and state, and then changed my identity. Every day henceforth I lived in fear of being 'done in'—all because of one terribly behaved toddler."

kids will also be the cause of a lot of unwanted toddler-related drama.

Most annoyingly, your toddler will imitate everything your older kid does. So, if your older kid flips out and throws a fit, you can bet your toddler will too. And if your older kid uses a bad word, your toddler will start saying it almost immediately. This will greatly amuse your older kid or kids, who will then teach your toddler every bad word and inappropriate song they know. You can always tell which toddler at the park has older siblings—she's the one teaching the others a new "F-word."

Your older kids will teach your toddler other ways to misbehave too. Do your older kids know how to sneak candy out of the candy drawer? If so, you can bet your toddler will learn soon enough. For a toddler, having an older sibling is like having a personal Mr. Miyagi, but for mischief instead of karate.

If all of that weren't bad enough, there will also be lots of screaming, yelling, and crying. When your toddler breaks one of your older kid's things (which will happen regularly) your older kid will have a meltdown in spectacular fashion. This, of course, will cause your toddler to melt down too. At other times your older kid will be the one causing the tears, especially when she decides to lock your toddler out of her room. To survive these moments you will need to have a calming mantra, such as "Keep it together, keep it together."

Thankfully, older kids can be reasoned with, or failing that, threatened effectively. The more you can inspire your older kid to be a good role model, either through positive reinforcement or by threatening to toss their Xbox into the ocean, the more (relatively) peaceful your home will be.

FUR SIBLINGS

Dogs and cats may not be people, technically speaking, but if you have one in the home you almost definitely think of yours as family. In fact, you may even refer to your pet as your "fur baby" (and not just after you've had a few too many cocktails). If you do have a dog or cat, your toddler will be interacting with her "fur sibling" on a daily basis, and like her dealings with her actual siblings, things are going to be bad before they get better.

In the early days of toddlerhood, your kid probably won't pay too much attention to your pet, but one day that will suddenly change in a major way. Your formerly inattentive toddler will dole out atomic hugs (that will feel like MMA chokeholds to your pet), pull on tails, wipe pancake syrup into fur, offer up less than pet-friendly fruit snacks to be eaten, and dress your pet like a Disney princess. If you have a small pet, your toddler will awkwardly carry your pet around until she drops your furry friend (or your pet leaps to safety like a Depression-era hobo jumping off a train). If you have a large pet, your toddler will use your pet for a seat or try to ride your pet like a horse. Your pet (who was accustomed to dozing lazily near your toddler) will now constantly be on edge and nap as far away from her as possible. If the sound of approaching toddler feet is heard, your pet will frantically seek higher ground (a.k.a. the couch). Basically, if your pet and your toddler were in a relationship, your pet would say, "I need some space," and your toddler would respond, "*But I love you!*"

TODDLER TIP #17

Always model proper pet care in front of your toddler. How you treat your pet will play a large role in how your toddler treats your pet.

If this sounds like a nightmare for you and your pet, that's because it is. The good news is there are things you can do to transition your toddler from a pet's worst nightmare into a slightly annoying but tolerable housemate. First, teach your toddler early on how to gently touch your pet, and say "Nice pet!" or "Gentle!" whenever she starts to get a little too rough. If your toddler does something to hurt your pet, make a show of comforting your pet in front of her, and calmly but firmly do your best to ensure that your toddler understands her actions hurt your pet. You should also take care not to leave your toddler and pet alone together until your toddler better understands how to interact with an animal. Even the most tolerant pet, when pushed too far, can scratch or nip.

Last, you must think twice before leaving your toddler within close proximity of your pet's food and water bowls. To your toddler's eyes, the water bowl isn't a water bowl, but a new toy! And your pet's food bowl, well, let's just say things only go downhill from there. So, do the safe thing and put your pet's food out of reach when you're out of the room.

VENTURING INTO PUBLIC

CHAPTER 6

During a state of emergency you're often advised to return to your home and take shelter there until further notice. Since having a toddler is more than a little like a state of emergency, staying at home until further notice (or until your kid is no longer a toddler) is a pretty good idea. However, there are times when you *will* need to venture into public with your toddler. This isn't for the faint of heart.

There will be tantrums. There will be potty accidents. There will be things that get broken. And then there will be all of the things that happen *after* you reach your destination. Ready for the really bad news? Every place you go—from the mall to the beach to the doctor's office—will come with its own set of problems you will have to deftly navigate to keep your toddler from ruining your day (and possibly week, month, and year). Ready to step outside? Let's go!

RESTAURANTS

Look, we get it. You *want* to eat out. You've been cooped up in your home listening to the Elmo song on repeat and subsisting on your toddler's leftover mac and cheese, and you need a break. But eating out with a toddler isn't anything like eating out without one. If you're hoping to relax, enjoy good conversation, and savor delicious food, you're going to be disappointed.

If, however, you're hoping to leave the restaurant even more stressed out than you were before you went in, then eating out with a toddler is definitely for you! The first thing you will have to deal with are all of the eyes. The eyes will belong to the other customers (and much of the wait staff) and they will silently warn you and your toddler not to ruin their night as you make the long, uncomfortable walk past them to your table.

Once you arrive at your table, you will need to immediately make it toddler friendly. If there are jam packets, for example, you will have to quickly hide them from your toddler. If you don't, and he spots them, you will find yourself in another kind of jam! You will also need to move any glasses of water out of his reach as well as any utensils (so he doesn't stab you with a fork or butter knife when he spots you hiding the jam).

Now under normal circumstances you might like to sit and unwind for a moment, leisurely perusing the menu. You absolutely cannot do this with a toddler. Instead, you must order immediately because a toddler at a restaurant is a ticking time bomb. It's not a matter of if he'll go off, but when. Many a regretful parent has staggered out of a restaurant mumbling, "The appetizer. We never should have ordered the appetizer!"

 Always bring cash so that if your toddler totally loses it you can drop a few bills onto the table and leave in a hurry.

You can also improve your chances of experiencing a moderately satisfying meal out by bringing toys, games, coloring books, and other diversions for your toddler. The more you engage your toddler, the less likely he will be to get out of hand. You should plan for your dinner conversation to be as much about Lightning McQueen and *Cars* as anything you and your partner actually want to discuss.

If you're thinking, "Pfft. I got this," you should know there are many other stressful things you will have to deal with— far more than we can go into here. For example, you may have to physically restrain your toddler for the entire meal because he's desperate to explore the restaurant. Or maybe he'll just want to explore under the table where he'll find and eat someone's two-day-old chicken finger. Will it make him seriously sick? Probably not. But you'll be up that night worrying about it anyway.

With all of this stress, it's easy to get into an argument with your partner, especially over who has to take your unruly toddler to walk around the parking lot and who gets to stay and enjoy their meal in glorious peace. Working out a fair trade ("I'll take this tantrum, you get the next!") is the best way to go, and this is far preferable to having a screaming match on the drive home.

In the end, while it is possible to enjoy eating out with your toddler under the right circumstances, it's also important to remember there's always takeout.

PARKS

If you absolutely must venture into public with your toddler, you could do a lot worse than the park. After all, it costs nothing to visit and will almost definitely tire out your toddler. He might even nap when you get back home, giving you the rare opportunity to use the bathroom in private or to finally watch that show everyone keeps talking about. Sounds good, right? Well, before you decide to make the park your home away from home, you should know that visiting one with a toddler is often not quite a "day at the park."

Parks tend to be wide-open spaces, which are great for dogs and soccer games, but not so great for your toddler. Why? Because at a park just about anything will make a toddler take off running. A butterfly? Sure! An ice cream truck? You betcha! An imaginary friend? Probably! Because of this, you must be poised to run and grab your toddler—who will suddenly move like a thirty-pound Usain Bolt—at all times.

When your toddler isn't darting off, he will probably be trying to climb the park's most dangerous jungle gym or slide. Basically, the more dangerous and inappropriate something is for your toddler, the more he will want to play on it. If you can, try to re-direct his attention to the swing. The swing may be monotonous to push, but it will contain your toddler and allow you to stare blankly into the distance without having to worry about what mischief he might be getting into. Sandboxes are also toddler-appropriate. If you bring sand toys like scoops, buckets, and dump trucks, your toddler will be more likely to stay put and play.

More than anything, though, you need to be wary of other people. Older kids, for example, will tear around the park with absolutely no regard for your toddler's safety. This will put him at risk of becoming the victim of a run-by knock-down. If your toddler blocks entry to a slide, he will be pushed aside, or worse—"nudged" down whether he's ready or not. You must also be sure he doesn't stray too close to the swings without you. If he does, your toddler might end up with a first grader's foot imprinted on his back.

The kids may be difficult, but their parents will be even worse. They will judge you if your toddler is too rough with the other kids, but also if he's a pushover. They will judge you if the snacks you feed him are unhealthy, but also if they're too healthy. And they'll judge you if you're on your phone too much, but also if you helicopter over your toddler. In short, you will feel like you are in high school again, and on most days you won't be able to wait for the bell to ring.

When you leave the park, make sure to blast your kid's favorite music on the way home so he doesn't fall asleep. The last thing you want is for him to sleep in the car and dash any chance of his napping at home. After all you endured at the park, your kid is going to nap at home (while you enjoy a well-deserved break) or nowhere at all.

THE BEACH

When you think about taking your toddler to the beach, do you imagine that classic Coppertone baby ad? Do you picture a strikingly blue ocean, palm trees swaying in the breeze, and your toddler reacting adorably when something surprising happens (like having his swim bottoms pulled down by a puppy)? If so, stop right now. That was an ad, and like most ads it was lying to you. The reality of taking a toddler to the beach is very different, and if a dog pulls down your toddler's swim shorts he won't react with good-natured bemusement, he'll shriek and need twenty minutes of consoling.

The first drama you'll have to deal with will be packing all of the stuff you'll need . . . which is a lot. Veteran parents may advise, "Be sure you don't overpack!" but if you notice they always follow that up with, "Of course, you'll need to bring a large beach bag, bug spray, hand sanitizer, a toddler-sized beach chair, a waffle iron, two snow globes . . ." The best plan is neither here nor there. You don't want to pack so much that you feel like you've turned into a one-person moving company, but you *really* don't want to get stuck out there without something that could keep your toddler from losing it. Sand toys, a cooler for snacks and drinks, and an umbrella are a few things you should consider as essentials.

 TODDLER TIP #19

If your toddler is newly potty trained, be sure to go to a beach that has a public bathroom and set up camp near it.

WHAT YOU DON'T WANT TO HEAR WHEN OUT AND ABOUT

1. "WHERE'S MY BLANKET?"

. . . as you're pushing the stroller out of Disneyland after eight hours at the park.

2. "WHY IS THAT MAN SO OLD?"

. . . after the man complimented you on your beautiful child.

3. "I WANT TO GO!"

. . . as you sit in your seats for the Sesame Street Live! show you dropped eighty bucks on.

4. "LOOK WHAT I GOT!"

. . . when you get back to the car and realize your toddler shoplifted a candy bar at the checkout.

5. "I'M HUNGRY!"

. . . after you threw away the food court quesadilla he sat in front of for thirty minutes without touching.

6. "YOU'RE MAKING STINKY POOPOO!"

. . . when you're in a stall in a crowded bathroom.

7. "OWWWW! YOU HURTING ME!"

. . . when you're trying to lead your kid out of a play area, trying not look like an early nominee for "Worst Parent of the Year."

8. "PICK ME UP!"

. . . when you're carrying three bags of groceries.

9. "UH-OH. BROKE IT."

. . . after you reluctantly let him use your phone.

10. "MY PANTS ARE WET!"

. . . anytime.

Next, after schlepping all of your gear onto the sand, you will have to deal with the Battle of the Sunscreen. Toddlers hate being slathered in the stuff and will do just about anything to stop you from applying it, but since their sensitive skin means they'll burn faster than Conan O'Brien covered in tanning oil, you'll need to apply it thoroughly despite your toddler's squirming, flying elbows, and pleas of "ALL DONE!"

After that, you'll finally be able to relax, right? Not so fast. You will need to be hyperaware of how your toddler responds to the ocean because he might run straight into it without any sense of self-preservation (meaning you will need to be hot on his tail). Most toddlers, however, are terrified of the ocean and don't want to go anywhere near it. If your toddler is one of them, be cool with it. There's really no upside to forcing him to "enjoy" the water, and having him play in the sand next to your blanket will seriously lower your stress levels.

At this point you will be able to relax (yay!) at least until your toddler starts complaining. If your toddler complains about being too hot, let him hang in the shade (thank you, umbrella), and if he complains about being too cold, put a sweatshirt on him (oh, yeah, you'll need to bring that too). There will also be lots of complaining about the sand. Your toddler may love playing in it, but he won't love getting it in his mouth, ears, eyes, and swimsuit. Thankfully, baby powder works wonders for getting sand off, so you'll definitely want to pack a travel-sized bottle.

The greatest antidote for complaining is food (and drinks, too, since the sun can be dehydrating). The odd thing is that toddlers are almost transcendently bad at eating at the beach. The average toddler will drop anywhere from one to five of his snacks onto the sand. To avoid suffering through a scene straight out of *The Birds*, have your toddler eat over a clean towel instead. You can even try putting your toddler's hands in disposable plastic bags or gloves when he's eating to limit the chances of him getting sand on his food.

When you're ready to pack up and go home, it's a good idea to have towels and a change of clothes waiting in the car so your toddler can freshen up. This will save you from having to listen to your toddler whine, "FEEL DOY-TOY! FEEL WET! WAH!" all the way home from your "relaxing" day at the beach.

MOVIE THEATERS

A few months into your kid's toddlerhood, an animated movie will come out about, say, an anthropomorphized ceiling fan, and you'll think, "How fun! I need to take the kid to see that!"

First, some things to consider. Movies are screened in the dark; toddlers tend to be afraid of the dark. Moviegoers need to sit still; toddlers act like every chair they sit on is on fire. Moviegoers are expected to be quiet; toddlers are, well . . . ! But you're brave, right? You're doing this! So, let's plan for success.

To start, you'll definitely want to plan to get into your seats as close to the start of the movie as possible. This is generally ten to fifteen minutes after the time printed on

TODDLER TIP #20

Many theaters offer "Mommy and Me" screenings where the house lights are left on during the screening and it's perfectly acceptable for your toddler to make a little noise. These are ideal for a toddler's first movie experience.

your ticket because of all the previews. I know, I know. You like to watch the previews. But you will only have so much time before your toddler loses interest (or flat-out loses it), so it's best to keep your trip to the movie theater as brief as possible.

Once you arrive you will need to understand that, to your toddler's eyes, the movie theater is a never-before seen, incredibly cool-looking wonderland. His first instinct will be to explore it, not sit on his butt. He will want to crawl under the theater's seats, run up and down the aisles, even stand in front of the audience and shake his booty. Alternatively, he might whine to return to the lobby, in order to check it out some more (especially if he saw it had video games). Unless you want to spend the entire second act of the talking ceiling fan movie trailing after your toddler in the lobby, you should avoid drawing your toddler's attention to the cool stuff on your way in.

From here, keeping your toddler in his seat will be key, and the best way to do this is by plying him with treats, either purchased at a king's ransom at the concession stand or by smuggling them inside in your biggest purse. Popcorn and healthy snacks are good because they aren't packed with sugar (and won't give your toddler a sugar rush thirty minutes before the end of the movie), but candy will work in a pinch.

Picking a screening time when your kid will be the least hyper (for instance, a little before he regularly naps) is smart. You can also help matters by bringing a small, quiet toy for your kid to hold.

Most importantly, keep your expectations low. Remind yourself going in that this will be the first of many movie experiences you'll have with your kid, and if this one doesn't work out, there will be better ones ahead. If things go south fast, you can always carry your screaming toddler back to the ticket booth for a refund. They should be able to take one look at the situation and gladly give you one.

THE DOCTOR'S OFFICE

The only thing worse than going to the doctor for yourself is having to take your toddler for a checkup. In fact, a recent poll found that nearly nine out of ten parents would rather suffer through a physical than take their toddler to the doctor. Unfortunately, there's no getting around these visits, but if you play your cards right you can survive with a portion of your sanity intact.

The first drama you'll have to deal with will involve the toys in the waiting room, which will most definitely be germ-infested. Your toddler will want to play with them, so you'll be forced to make one of those not-fun-at-all parenting choices: let him play with the toys and expose him to a who's who of cold and flu viruses (but keep him calm and happy), or forbid him from touching them, thereby avoiding the germs but almost definitely guaranteeing a meltdown long before you see the doctor. This is a great reason to include wipes and hand sanitizer in your supply bag (and don't forget to remind your kid to avoid touching his face while he plays). Another potential solution is to bring small toys from home to keep him busy with instead of the radioactive ones.

When the nurse finally calls you back there's a very strong chance your toddler will freak out, especially if he's been there before. This is because your toddler's selective memory will be on glorious display at the doctor's office. That shot, blood draw, or uncomfortable exam he received at his last visit? He'll remember it like it happened five minutes ago. But the toy or lollipop he received at the end of that visit? That's long forgotten. To soothe your toddler's nerves, it's a good idea to be ready to whip out prized toys or other distractions when you hear the words, "The doctor is ready to see you now."

The exam room also comes with its own host of problems. There's no shortage of cabinets and drawers for your toddler to get into, the scale and the blood pressure cuffs will fascinate him, and if he sees the tongue depressors you'll have to hear him whine for a popsicle. On the plus side, if there's one item that mesmerizes every toddler, it's the exam table paper. Toddlers love the way it sounds, the way it crinkles, and the way it rips. Ask the nurse if it's okay

 TODDLER TIP #21 The best time to schedule appointments is right after meals so your toddler isn't hungry and cranky.

for your toddler to draw on the paper with crayons—this will keep him too distracted to be destructive.

Lastly, toddlers often suffer from White Coat Syndrome—when they see the pediatrician, they immediately lose it and clam up. Watching your normally boisterous and talkative toddler sit there in silence can be incredibly frustrating, and force you to weakly claim, "He talks so much at home, I swear!" If there's something your toddler is doing that you specifically want the doc to see, film it at home on your cell phone as opposed to expecting him to do it on command at the doctor's office.

RECORDED TODDLER DYSFUNCTION THROUGHOUT HISTORY

In 2000, *Gladiator*, a historical drama set in 180 AD about the gladiatorial battles of Rome, won Best Picture at the Academy Awards and grossed nearly $500 million worldwide. The original draft of the screenplay, however, featured many scenes that failed to make it into the final film. One of these scenes—a dramatization of a passage the film's historian found in a little-known history book written in 187 AD—is reproduced below:

EXT. COLOSSEUM ARENA - DAY
Maximus stands at the end of the tunnel leading into the arena, waiting his turn to fight, as two gladiators—the hulking HERMINIOUS and overmatched RUFUS—battle.

HERMINIOUS
Hades awaits, but not for me!

Herminious swings his sword, sending Rufus stumbling backward, and the CROWD rises, YELLING. Encouraged, Herminious attacks Rufus again and again until the smaller man falls to one knee. Herminious raises his sword, ready to deliver the death blow, when the SHRILL CRY of a child rises above the din. Herminious looks into THE CROWD . . . where a stressed-out mother and father struggle to quiet a toddler who is having a full-blown tantrum. The other spectators glare at them, annoyed.

IN THE ARENA
  . . . *Herminious lowers his sword and scowls.*

HERMINIOUS
A toddler? Here? Who would bring a toddler to
something like this? That's just terrible parenting!

Rufus, taking advantage of the distraction, leaps up and sinks his sword into Herminious. Herminious staggers, then uses his last bit of strength to turn back toward the crowd.

HERMINIOUS
Take that toddler home! You should be ashamed
of yourselves!

Herminious collapses, dead, and the crowd's response is DEAFENING . . . but not so deafening that it drowns out the cries of the toddler.

THE DENTIST'S OFFICE

Compared to the hair-pulling stress of a trip to the doctor's office, a trip to the pediatric dentist's office is relatively easy. Of course, since we're talking about toddlers, the emphasis here is on *relatively*.

Picking the right dentist is the single most important thing you can do to make sure things go smoothly. Making the right decision, though, has very little to do with whether the dentist is any good. This is because any dentist you take your toddler to will (presumably) be licensed—and besides, at this stage they do little more than count your toddler's teeth and provide a light cleaning. No, what you will need to be on the lookout for is a fun, kid-friendly dentist. Does the office seem more like a play place than a medical office? If so, you've probably made the right choice. On the other hand, if the place is cold and sterile and the dentist looks like he should have retired a quarter-century ago, you probably should keep looking.

Your toddler will still be a little wary of the dentist even if the exam chair looks like it would be at home in a Toys "R" Us aisle. Toddlers are like animals, and they can smell the fear coming off of the older, more experienced kids in the office. And, despite their best efforts, dentists and hygienists can still look scary behind their masks. Luckily, dentists are used to causing yelps of fear. She may even take the opportunity to count your kid's teeth while his mouth is in a wide-open scream.

You will also need to prepare yourself for the stress of having to be your toddler's straightjacket during teeth cleanings. Toddlers, knowing your weakness, will often yell out, "No, mommy, no!" Or even, "Save me, daddy!" This would rattle even Captain Georg von Trapp, so to unwind the stress afterward, and to get back into the good graces of your toddler, take him out for ice cream. Just be sure to make yours a double—you'll need it.

PLAY AREAS

Visiting a play area (or "germ factory" as you will soon come to know them) is a little like betting all of your money on red at a roulette table. If you're lucky and the ball lands on red, you will win twenty minutes to sit on a bench and a toddler who might actually nap later! But if the ball bounces around another second and lands on black, your toddler will come down with a cold a day or two later, and that's a fate much worse than losing your shirt in Vegas.

If it were up to your toddler, though, he would risk it every time because he won't see the all-toddler cast of *Contagion* milling about—all he'll see are the slides, plastic animals, and that sweet, sweet ball pit. So, if you don't want to risk being up at 3:00 a.m. with a sick and whiny toddler for the next week, you'd be wise to take precautions. Not sure where the play area is in the new mall you're visiting? You'd better find out and make plans to steer clear of it (way clear) because if your toddler gets even the most distant glimpse of those plastic animals there will be no leaving without a visit, epic tantrum, or both.

CHAPTER 6

Of course, it won't matter how many precautions you take. The odds are you will end up visiting at least a few play areas, either because someone will invite you to a play date at one of those indoor places that charge admission (basically the toddler version of a night club), your toddler will wear you down at the mall, or you will blow into a fast food restaurant without realizing (gasp!) it has a play place. In these situations, you will need plenty of wipes and you will need to be on the lookout for:

- **Toddler-on-toddler combat:** One second all of the toddlers will be playing well together, then the next the ball pit will be transformed into a cage match. You'll definitely want to be ready to pull your toddler to safety at the drop of a juice box.

- **Top-of-the-slide pileups:** A toddler or two will often decide that, instead of going down the slide, they're just going to hang out at the top of it! This won't, however, stop the other toddlers from trying to go down the slide. No, they will keep climbing to the top of the slide until—like a jammed assembly line—everyone goes toppling down the chute.

- **Your toddler trying to take a toy into the play area:** How's this for a nightmare scenario? You're about to leave when your toddler yells, "I lost my Buzz Lightyear!" You then look into the play area and realize . . . it could be *anywhere*. At the bottom of the ball pit? Maybe. In one of the tunnels twenty feet in the air? Could be! Already swiped by some no-good kid? Who knows! But you will have to spend the

123

next hour looking for it regardless. Thankfully, you can avoid this particular horror by insisting your toddler leave his stuff with you.

- **Your toddler getting "lost in space":** This is especially problematic at fast food play areas where toddlers crawl/climb to the top of the structure, then freak out upon realizing how high they are and refuse to come down. You can coo, "It's okay, buddy! Come on down!" as much as you want, but you will more than likely have to go up there after him. Trying to squeeze your way to the top with a burger, jumbo fries, and shake in your belly is no one's idea of a good time—and the closest you will come to re-experiencing your own birth.

Oh, and know that your kid will lose it when you say it's time to go no matter how long you've been there. So be prepared to carry a screaming toddler to the exit. The other parents may stare, but take heart: their time will come very, very soon.

THE SUPERMARKET

In the month or two before your kid becomes a full-fledged toddler you will likely find going to the supermarket relatively easy. Just strap your kid into the cart, hand him a toy, and get shopping! Sure, he might have the occasional crying jag or inopportune dirty diaper, but at this stage you won't have to bite back tears at the mere thought of bringing him with you. That, however, will all change once you have a toddler.

The most frustrating thing about trying to shop with a toddler is that he will most likely refuse to stay in the (insert expletive of choice) shopping cart. In fact, you might not be able to even get him *in* the cart since many toddlers kick, scream, and arch their backs the moment you lift them

TODDLER TIP #22 Be sure to learn where the candy, cookies, and toys are located at your local supermarket so you can plan to take the least tantrum-inducing route possible.

in the air. When this happens you will have two options. You can give up and set your toddler down (and deal with the consequences when you get inside), or you can fight to strap your toddler in while trying not to get clocked by his flailing arms and feet—all in front of the watchful eyes of cookie-selling Girls Scouts and judgmental shoppers.

It should be mentioned that even if you do manage to get your toddler into the cart, he will likely whine to be let out almost immediately upon getting inside the store. And why wouldn't he? The supermarket is full of balloons, candy, cookies, ice cream, and toys. It's basically a toddler paradise, and no toddler wants to watch it all pass by while stuck in the cart. With that said, you can (and should) attempt to keep your little monster content with being in the cart by engaging him with a song, giving him a toy, or even ripping open a can of Pringles and letting him go to town (just ignore the side-eye from the stock boy). If you're really desperate you can give him your phone, but this isn't recommended because when your toddler is worked up he will be able to toss it an Olympic-record distance.

If you're unable to stop your toddler from whining to get out, you can make the game-time decision to ignore his pleas and simply go about your shopping. If you do this, though, you should know that he will scream louder every second he is confined to the cart. Most parents break and let their toddler down after a minute of shrieking, or when glass bottles start rattling on the shelves—whichever comes first.

While letting your toddler down will stop him from screaming, it will also put you in an even worse situation— shopping with an unrestrained toddler! When you're not struggling to keep your toddler from running out of sight, you'll be making him put back candy and cookies or whispering for him to stop staring at the awkward college kid perusing the ramen noodles.

One thing you can do to keep your free-range toddler in check is to make him your "helper." Try asking him to bring you easy-to-carry items like paper towels (but not eggs or cartons of milk), and let him "help" you push the cart. Just don't let him push it by himself or you will definitely hear, "Cleanup on aisle three!"

The best way to prepare for shopping with a toddler is by realizing these trips will be chaotic, stressful, and potentially embarrassing, and be okay with it. That's because when your kid is being especially maddening (say, after shattering a glass of juice and screaming "WANT CANDY!" repeatedly) you will be tempted to scoop him up and make a break for the exit. Doing that, though, means you will have to come back again later, most likely with your toddler. Forget that. Instead of putting off the misery for later, stay calm and continue shopping with your little maniac. Other shoppers may shoot you looks, but who cares? If dealing with a few sideways glances means you're able to get everything you need (plus the wine you're going to drink that night while watching some hard-earned TV), so be it.

VACATIONING
WITH A TODDLER

CHAPTER 7

When you think *vacation* you might picture sandy beaches. You can see it now: you and your partner soaking up the sun, relaxing, with a rum drink in hand. Was that fun? I hope so, because that little daydream is as close as you're going to get to the picture-perfect vacation. Toddlers change everything, no matter the location. You may get poolside. You may visit with friends or family. But the truth is that we just can't recommend vacationing with a toddler—at least not if you plan to think of it as a typical vacation.

Just look at the numbers. Parents who vacation with a toddler are up to thirty-seven times more likely to suffer a toddler-induced breakdown than parents who remain at home with their toddlers. (This number nearly doubles among those who vacation at an amusement park, but more on that later.) If you absolutely must vacation with a toddler, it is better to think of it as "traveling" instead of "vacationing" because it will afford you little joy or relaxation. Ready? Strap yourself and your toddler in. Here we go!

FLYING

The classic airline slogan may invite you to "come fly the friendly skies," but when you have a toddler you must be prepared to fly the unfriendly skies instead. No, parents of toddlers don't sit back, relax, and enjoy their flight; they spend every second paranoid that their kid will lose it while trapped in a confined space. Thankfully, there are measures you can take to limit your chances of receiving an epic stink-eye in baggage claim upon landing.

Takeoff can be especially painful on a toddler's ears, so as you ascend you should give your toddler milk, juice, or water to drink. Unfortunately, because you can't bring liquid through security, you will have to buy these drinks in the terminal at movie theater prices. The investment is worth it, though, as a drink will help alleviate your toddler's pain and stop crotchety (or already drunk passengers) from shouting, "Shut that kid up!"

To keep your toddler content once you're in the air, you will want to bring a backpack (it can be your toddler's carry-on) full of things like a security blanket, tablet, child-friendly headphones, and small toys. Surprising your toddler with a few new trinkets bought in the dollar section will buy you precious tantrum-free time, as will DIYing some crafts you've found on Pinterest. A handmade toy made out of pipe cleaners may seem silly in the comfort of your own home, but when your toddler is melting down at thirty-thousand feet you'll soon be thinking *why didn't I make that stupid toy out of pipe cleaners?!*

Snacks are another thing that can keep your toddler busy for a surprisingly long time, but you will want to bring these from home and not rely on what is on the flight. If you think airline food is unappetizing, just imagine what a picky toddler will think.

Of course, the real challenge is the balancing act of keeping your toddler happy while making sure she doesn't bother other passengers by kicking the seat in front her, making loud noises, or staring horror film–style through the seats at the people behind her. Be warned, though: you must check your toddler carefully because each rebuke increases the odds of a meltdown.

TODDLER TIP #23

If someone yells "Shut that kid up!" use the opportunity to win the sympathy of your fellow passengers by acting hurt instead of angry—if possible, summon tears.

In the likely event that your toddler does melt down after you've done everything you possibly can to keep her calm, there are a few last-ditch strategies you can employ, like feigning shock at how your toddler is acting. Try theatrically saying things like, "She's never like this!" or "It must be the altitude. That's the only possible explanation!"

It's also helpful to make a show of continuing to do everything you can to calm your toddler even though you know she's well past the point of no return. Will it make a difference? No. But if you don't do your best Meryl Streep in the role of "The Tireless, Overwhelmed Parent" the people around you will hate you—and you've still got three hours before you land. You may have given up in your heart, but you can't show it on the outside.

If the flight attendant isn't avoiding you, you can try asking him to bring you some extra milk, cookies, or anything else that might possibly placate your toddler. If he says he can't help you, try to slip him a twenty like he's a maître d' at a fancy restaurant.

If all else fails, you can become the sad sack parent who endlessly walks your toddler up and down the aisles. This should only be done out of desperation, though, because once your toddler knows she can get out of her seat she will never want to get back in.

Once you master all that, prepare to join the Mile High Club for parents. This is very different from the Mile High Club the honeymooners a few aisles ahead might join. To join the parent's club, you must successfully change a diaper in the tiny airplane bathroom. This is quite the challenge, but you can make the experience less miserable

CHANGE A DIAPER AT 36,000 FEET

1 WAIT IN LINE.

2 CRAM YOURSELF INSIDE.

3 CHANGE DIAPER AMIDST TURBULENCE.

by pretending that you and your toddler are giants forced to live among humans. Just don't mention this to anyone else—it's best kept a secret.

ROAD TRIPS

After thinking about the travails of air travel, the idea of simply packing your toddler into the car and hitting the road may seem like a no-brainer. However, when you find yourself three hundred miles from your destination and your toddler is still shrieking because you didn't stop at a McDonald's, you will realize that road trips come with their own set of sanity-testing challenges, not the least of which is that they tend to take three to four times longer than a flight to the same location. If you're not careful, your drive can very easily drive you nuts.

The most difficult part of any road trip will undoubtedly be keeping your toddler happy. Since toddlers aren't impressed by scenery or the back of their parents' heads, the parent in the passenger seat will likely need to spend the majority of the trip turned around, playing the role of activities director. ("That concludes our juice box portion of the drive. Next up . . . an iPad presentation of Elmo's World!") The good news is that many of the strategies discussed in the previous section, like having a backpack full of toys and lots of snacks on hand, will help to keep your toddler busy on a road trip too. You will also have one major advantage over those who fly: you'll be in the privacy of your own car. This means you can do things to entertain your toddler that you wouldn't dare do in front of another human being. Improvised songs about butts? Sure! Woefully inept impressions of Mickey Mouse? Knock yourself out! Fake fart noises? Of course! You should feel free to do all of these things and more without worrying about what other people would think. Your only concern should be whether they entertain your toddler.

Another trying part of road trips is that your toddler will repeatedly drop things she can't pick up while strapped into his car seat. Since these will be things she *absolutely must have right now*, you will either need to pull over to get them (losing precious time) or reach into the back "go-go gadget" style to pick them up. While the latter is preferable because it saves time, you want to make sure you don't pull a muscle, or pull right off the road, in the process.

It's possible to pull a muscle while changing your toddler's diapers, because most diaper changes on road trips (such as the almost impossible "standing change" in a nasty, changing table–free gas station bathroom) are firmly in the high difficulty range. To escape these situations with as little trauma as possible, you will want to bring a travel-changing pad or kit and antibacterial hand sanitizer (plus plenty of diapers and wipes, of course).

In addition to making stops for diaper changes, you'll want to consider making occasional stops at rest stops, restaurants, and roadside attractions. These will add time

If people in another car notice you doing something embarrassing to entertain your toddler, slow down so they can drive ahead and out of sight.

RECORDED TODDLER DYSFUNCTION THROUGHOUT HISTORY

The logs of Christopher Jones, captain of the Mayflower on its historic trip to the New World in 1620, includes the following entry:

"THE 12TH OF AUGUST, 1620

Morale among the passengers is low. The source of this malaise is a babe of two or three years. Yesterday at daybreak he shattered the first mate's telescope by savagely throwing it to the ground, at noon he angered the cook by overturning a plate of food ('No carrot!' the child is said to have uttered), and at night his wailing tormented the other passengers, one of whom shouted, 'Lo! Silence that child up!' The boy's mother, meanwhile, shuffled across the deck with dazed eyes, pleading with anyone to watch the boy so that she might have but a moment of peace. Only one among us, a crewman able to summon the sound of flatulence from his armpit, was able to render the child anything but incorrigible. Even now, as I write, I can hear the terror wailing below. We cannot arrive in the New World soon enough."

to your trip, but they will give both you and your toddler a welcome respite from the car. You should know, though, that getting your toddler back into the car will take a lot of effort because once she's out she won't want to get back in. To avoid embarrassment as you struggle to get your bucking toddler back into the car seat, it's important to remember you will never see the old ladies and truckers giving you side-eye at the rest stop ever again.

HOTELS

You likely have many positive memories of hotel stays from your pre-toddler life, full of rest, relaxation, and romance. Our best advice is to forget them.

Upon arriving you will need to immediately babyproof your room. This sounds easy, but babyproofing a hotel room goes well beyond simply covering sharp corners and electrical outlets. First, you must consider the mini bar. If it has a key, lock it, or else your toddler will pull out all of the items when you're not looking and roll a few fourteen dollar mini-bottles of booze under the couch (something you'll only discover upon reviewing your bill). Similarly, if there's a basket of candies, cookies, and chips atop the minibar, you will need to distract your toddler—pointing and shouting, "Look! Elmo!" is generally effective, then hurriedly stash it out of sight on the highest shelf in the closet. Fail to do so without your toddler noticing and she will spend the entirety of your stay whining, "Cookies! Cookies! Cookies!"

You will also need to make sure that the television controller is out of your toddler's reach. Toddlers love to push buttons and can quickly button-push their way into ordering a twenty-dollar on-demand movie (or worse—an adult movie). Explaining to the front desk that you "didn't really mean" to order *Debbie Does Dallas* while also claiming that you "honestly don't know what happened" to those mini-bottles of booze is best avoided.

Once you've made your hotel room hospitable to your toddler, you must go about the highly stressful task of staying in it. Why is this stressful, you ask? Let's count the ways:

1. There's no food for your toddler: Okay, there is food for toddlers at a hotel, but unless you've recently won the lottery you're probably not going to want to spend eight dollars for a bag of chips or seventeen dollars for a grilled cheese from room service (along with a thimble-sized glass of milk for four dollars). To avoid bankruptcy you should pack (or pick up at a local market) a bunch of toddler-friendly food.

2. There's nothing there to entertain her: While your toddler has toys to preoccupy herself at home, the most exciting "toy" in a hotel room is the "Do Not Disturb" sign. So, unless you want to work overtime to keep your toddler entertained ("Look, Honey, Mrs. Do Not Disturb Sign invited over Mr. Overpriced Water Bottle for a tea party!"), you're better off bringing toys, books, and games to keep your toddler busy.

3. Everything is white and/or immaculate: The curtains, bedspreads, sheets, pillows, towels, and a whole lot of other pristine items in the room will not mix well with your toddler, who makes more stains before breakfast than most people make in a year. You'd be wise to befriend the housekeeper, and to remember when things get really sticky that the fraternity brothers two floors down are probably doing way worse.

TODDLER TIP #25

If you remove the stocked items from a mini-bar, you can refrigerate milk and other healthy snacks for your toddler.

DEALING WITH THE FRONT DESK

If the front desk does call with a noise complaint at 4:00 a.m., it's best to acknowledge the noise and apologize. It is not recommended to engage in conversations like this:

FRONT DESK: "Ma'am, we've received a number of noise complaints —"
YOU: "Yes, I was just about to call myself. The party is very loud."
FRONT DESK: "Party?"
YOU: "Hmm-hmm. College kids next door."
FRONT DESK: "Ma'am, the complaints were about a screaming child."
YOU: "Really? I don't hear anything like that."
FRONT DESK: "Ma'am, I can hear the child coming over the line from your room."
YOU: "No, that's music from the party.
FRONT DESK: "Ma'am, I now hear the child crying, 'Mommy! Mommy!'"
YOU: "Are you sure the hotel isn't haunted?"
FRONT DESK: "I'm sending someone up."
YOU: "..."
FRONT DESK: "Ma'am?"
YOU: "I'm sorry. Having a toddler is just so, so hard. We'll keep things down."
(click)

4. You're in close proximity to other people: This means you will spend your entire stay fretting that your toddler will start screaming in the middle of the night. If your toddler does lose it at 4:00 a.m., the frantic moments you'll spend struggling to quiet her (as your neighbors grumble through the paper-thin walls) will sadly end up among the most memorable of your trip. In times like these it's important to remind yourself that with a toddler you are not "vacationing," but "traveling," especially if the front desk calls.

HOTEL POOLS

Spend enough time in the hotel room with your toddler bouncing off the walls and you will eventually find yourself saying, "Hey! Let's take her to the pool!" Before you do that, though, make sure you're prepared.

First, toddlers have delicate skin that burns easily, so you will need to lather yours up with an endless amount of sunscreen before you do anything else. You will spend so much time struggling to apply the stuff to your squirming toddler, in fact, that you will likely forget to apply it to yourself and wake up the next morning as red as a beet.

Next, you will need to put your toddler into a swim diaper even though no one actually knows what the purpose of a swim diaper is since it doesn't hold or stop pee. Because of this, you should be prepared for your toddler to pee on you as you make your way to the pool.

Upon arriving at the pool it will be time to unpack the water toys you brought, but you must be prepared for your toddler to ignore them. She will, however, desperately want the toy some stranger's kid is playing with in the vicinity.

Finally, you and your toddler will get into the pool where she will either immediately scream to get out or splash around in ecstasy. While the latter is cute, be warned: if your toddler takes to the water, she will scream bloody murder when you try to leave no matter how long you've stayed at the pool. To avoid embarrassment, it's best to avoid eye contact with others as you hurry your wailing banshee out of the pool and back to your room.

VISITING RELATIVES

One of the most common reasons parents subject themselves to traveling with a toddler is to visit far-flung relatives. After all, what could be more magical than seeing the look on your great aunt's face when she meets your toddler for the first time? Unfortunately, these visits rarely end on such a magical note. The last look you're likely to see on your relative's face is one of great relief.

The main reason these visits go so poorly is simple. Before you arrive, the only image your great aunt knows of your toddler is the finely crafted one you've presented on Facebook. She's seen the adorable snapshot of him smelling flowers (but not the tantrum he threw seconds later when you wouldn't let him rip the flowers out of the ground); she's watched the achingly sweet video of him cooing, "I love you, mommy!" (but not the part you cut out where green sludge trickled out of his nose); and she's laughed at the funny anecdote you shared about your toddler's love of music (but not the story you didn't share about how he savagely snapped your original vinyl record of "Thriller" in two). This will all change, though, once you arrive and your

great aunt not only sees him in the flesh, but meets him when he's out of his element from traveling.

Instead of trying to keep up the charade that your toddler is a perfect angel (and greatly stressing yourself out in the process), it's best to simply accept upfront that your aunt's image of your toddler is going to be epically shattered, and that, upon returning home, you will hear whisperings through the family grapevine that your kid is "a handful."

Another problem you will experience when visiting relatives is that very few of their homes are babyproofed. This means that as you discuss your great aunt's recent knee surgery, you will need to hover over your toddler so he doesn't run into a sharp corner or break the antique vase your aunt has displayed at toddler-eye level. To avoid potential disasters, it's a good idea to bring a travel babyproofing kit to cover up the most dangerous corners, and to ask if you can move any fragile items out of your toddler's reach. Don't be shy—these are your relatives, after all, and they don't want your kid to break their stuff either.

The last problem you must be prepared for comes from the relatives themselves. All relatives (especially grandparents) enjoy spoiling toddlers, often with candies and treats. To avoid returning to your hotel with a sugar-crazed toddler intent on loudly melting down throughout the night, you will need to play the villain and say things like, "Sorry, pal, grandpa didn't mean to give you that third chocolate bar. You've had enough." Your toddler will lose it, of course, but better now than later, at your hotel room.

AMUSEMENT PARKS

When planning a family vacation with a toddler, an amusement park seems like the perfect destination. After all, it checks off all of the toddler-friendly boxes: fun rides, delicious food, and costumed characters. Unfortunately, these are the very things that will have your toddler crying in front of thousands of people shortly after entering the gates.

In order to survive an amusement park, you would be wise to think of it not as a place designed to entertain your toddler, but to antagonize her. Don't believe it? Consider the things your toddler will come across:

1. Loud music, flashing lights, and costumed characters: This sensory overload will immediately greet your toddler upon entering and throw her off her game. And if a guy in a seven-foot-tall Shrek costume sneaks up and startles her, you might as well turn around and go home right then. Game, set, match to the amusement park.

2. Sugary food: Virtually every food sold inside is drenched in sugar, so unless you refuse to buy your toddler any treats (a decision she will not take well) she will spend her entire visit riding one sugar high and crash after the next.

3. Long lines: There are exasperatingly long lines for everything, and you'll have to work overtime to keep your instant gratification–craving toddler from melting down as you snake your way through them.

4. The hordes of hucksters: Every ten feet your toddler will pass someone hawking a shiny object or treat. A toddler can only handle so much of this temptation before she dissolves into a "WANT! WANT! WANT!" meltdown.

The best way to protect yourself against this onslaught of agitation is to postpone your visit until your kid has transitioned out of toddlerhood. But if you absolutely must go now, it's wise to have the lowest of expectations, and the understanding that even those are unlikely to be met. You may have a dream of getting an adorable snapshot of your toddler with, say, Mickey Mouse, but if she's freaked out by an adult-sized mouse walking around you will have to forget about that photo opp. Similarly, you should be prepared to wait an hour for a ride only to have your toddler freak out at the last minute and refuse to get on it. Maddening? Only if your expectations are more than an inch off the ground.

You will also need to be prepared for your toddler to not only be afraid of the stuff you expect, but the stuff you'd never think of, like the innocent, toddler-friendly boat ride through a sparkling musical wonderland. So, instead of forcing your toddler to do the things you want her to do, let her find the things she's comfortable with. If she loves the carousel and wants to ride it over and over, let her. You brought her so that she could enjoy herself, right? This, of

 TODDLER TIP #26 Always bring a stroller—even if your toddler won't sit in it—because you can use it to wheel around your stuff. And with a toddler, you will have stuff.

course, means that anything you, the adult, might personally want to do is almost definitely out of the question. Sure, you can go on a thrill ride by yourself, but that means leaving your partner alone with your sugar-crazed toddler, which is tantamount to cruel and unusual punishment. For the sake of your relationship, it's best to save the adult fun for future visits.

Lastly, you can make it a lot easier to get through your visit by bribing. Upon arriving, tell your toddler she can buy a souvenir—but at the end of your visit. That way, you won't have to schlep an oddly-shaped souvenir around all day and you'll avoid the drama of your toddler discovering something she wants more later in the day. Plus, the promise of a souvenir at the end of the visit is a highly effective good behavior motivator.

SURVIVING BEDTIME AND POTTY TRAINING

CHAPTER 8

When you're an adult, you love sleeping and can't get enough of it. And (if we're speaking frankly) you also probably enjoy a trip to the bathroom. But do toddlers enjoy these things? No, they do not. Tell a toddler it's bedtime, or suggest that she start to use the potty like a big kid, and the little weirdo will almost certainly burst into tears like you've just tossed her favorite stuffed animal into the blender and hit "puree."

By now, though, it should come as no surprise that toddlers are strange and irrational. It should also come as no surprise that it will be your job to: A) establish a bedtime routine for your toddler, and B) potty train her, even as she fights you every step of the way. Will it be easy? Not even remotely! Will it be fun? Gosh, no! But it has to be done. And try to log a few memories for comparison; in ten years, your kid will sleep in until eleven and spend thirty minutes in the bathroom at a time.

ANNOUNCING IT'S BEDTIME

At the end of a long day, you will want nothing more than to get your kid down for the night so you can enjoy a little toddler-free relaxation. That's perfectly understandable, but you mustn't put the horse before the cart. Getting your toddler to sleep is a process, and you must commit to it. If you don't—if you cut corners or race through the steps—you will likely find yourself crying at 11:00 p.m. as your wide-awake toddler acts out the last verse of "Five Little Monkeys."

The first step of the process is so important we're giving it its own entry in this book. You absolutely must announce that it's bedtime. Think of yourself as the town crier with news you must share early and often.

That doesn't mean the sole citizen of Toddler Town will like the news you're spreading. To keep your toddler from totally losing it, try letting her know ahead of time that bedtime is coming by saying, "Bedtime in twenty minutes, sweetie!" After you've made this first announcement, try to wind things down by transitioning to quieter activities. Put away that drum kit your sister-in-law gave her (why, oh why did you even keep it?!) and turn off any loud cartoons. As your toddler settles down, remind her every five minutes that bedtime is coming until it finally arrives. Your toddler probably won't waltz off to bed whistling a happy tune, but the odds are she will put up less of a fight if she can see what's around the bend, especially if you do this every night at the same time.

Your toddler's main strategy for fighting the news that it's bedtime will be to put on a one-toddler rendition of the "good cop/bad cop" routine. First, she will play the good toddler, and stall by batting her eyes adorably and asking for more cuddles. ("No bedtime, mama. More cuddles pwease.") Alternatively, she might look up at you with doleful eyes and say, "I'm hungry, daddy." Since you did feed her dinner, don't fall for this. If you do, you'll be stuck watching her nurse a handful of fishies for the next forty-five minutes.

If the good toddler doesn't sway you, she will quickly switch over to bad toddler. The bad toddler will cry, scream, attack, hide, and create any mischief that might make you throw up your hands and say, "Fine! Five more minutes!" But don't fall for this. Instead, stay strong and know that there will be nights when you have to take your toddler screaming and crying to the next step towards bed. Repeat your routine long enough, though, and those nights will become fewer and fewer. (Probably.)

THE BATHROOM ROUTINE

Once you've sufficiently warned your toddler about bedtime, it's time to usher her to the bathroom. Just getting her there might make you think, "Mission accomplished!" That, however, would be a major mistake because your toddler has not yet accepted defeat. In fact, she will continue to do absolutely everything in her power to derail the bedtime routine and make you scream, "I JUST WANT TO WATCH SOME TELEVISION WHERE PEOPLE SWEAR AND MAKE QUESTIONABLE DECISIONS! IS THAT SO MUCH TO ASK?"

TODDLER TIP #27

You can lessen toddler anxiety (and speed up the bedtime routine) by keeping the order of what your toddler does in the bathroom consistent night after night.

But don't do that. The most important thing to remember is to keep your cool (or to fake it). This will be a lot harder than you think because your toddler will suddenly become incapable of doing the simplest of tasks, or if she can do them, she will only be able to do them at a sloth-like speed. If you ask her to turn on the faucet, she'll reach for it like she's afraid it might run away if she moves too fast.

Your toddler will also do a lot of playing. She will splash in the water, push down the soap dispenser again and again, and use her toothbrush as a magic wand, sword, baseball bat, or drumstick (because all of this is apparently a lot more fun than going to bed). Again, we must stress how crucial it is that you keep your cool. The imminent threat of bedtime will have your toddler's emotions on edge, and if you snap at her she will likely burst into tears (and possibly flop onto the bathroom floor).

As far as a recommended order goes, if your toddler is potty trained, have her go to the bathroom. After that, have her wash her hands and face, then brush her teeth. If (or shall we say "when") she dillydallies, gently but firmly prompt her to keep moving by saying things like, "Okay, that's enough! Turn off the water!" or "Keep going! Don't stop!"

Think of yourself like a bartender getting the last drunk out of the bar at the end of a long night. You're not going to do anything that might antagonize her, but you are going to move her out so you can lock up and go home (or, in this case, move her into her bedroom so you can finally watch your shows).

THE BEDROOM ROUTINE

At this point, the only thing that separates you from freedom is the bedtime routine itself, or as it might better be described, the toddler's last stand. Your toddler will know that once you tuck her in and turn off the light she will be expected to sleep, so she will do everything in her power to make this part of the night last as long as possible. How you respond to her stalling tactics will be the difference between getting to enjoy the rest of your night and waking up on the floor of your toddler's bedroom at 2:00 a.m.

Above all else, you must stick to your routine and keep things moving. First, put your toddler into her pajamas, then quickly pivot to the bedtime story. If you don't expertly stick the landing of this maneuver, she will try to distract you by begging for a piggyback ride, starting a tickle fight, or ordering you to watch her do some somersaults.

If this does happen, channel Nancy Reagan: "Just say no." Yes, we know she was talking about drugs when she said that, but she was a mom, too, so she'd likely have agreed with us on this. If you go along with the piggyback ride/ tickle fight/tumbling exhibition, you'll not only lengthen the bedtime routine, you'll risk riling up your toddler enough to give her a second wind. There is not much *worse* for bedtime than a second wind.

You will also need to have a no-nonsense, full-speed ahead attitude when it comes to the bedtime story. Don't let your toddler strong-arm you into reading a painfully long book, don't let her constantly stop your reading by asking a dozen questions on every page, and when you get to the end of the book, don't be swayed by her cries of, "Again!" or "One more story!" Now is the time to close the book, plant your kisses, and move away from the bed.

Last but not least, you mustn't allow yourself to get stuck in your toddler's room. She will likely ask you to wait in her room until she falls asleep, or if she's feeling really bold, request that you cuddle her to sleep. She may look adorable when she asks you to do this as she tells you a woefully sad tale about being afraid of the monsters in her closet, but you will need to shut that down. If you don't, you will find yourself trapped in the ultimate time suck. For five, ten, fifteen, sometimes twenty minutes or more, you will do nothing but stare at your toddler searching for any sign that she might have nodded off. And if you try to tiptoe out before she's totally asleep and get caught ("Mama? Dada? Where you goin'?"), she will force herself to stay up as long as possible afterward to make sure you don't try to sneak out again. You will literally be held captive by your toddler.

 If your toddler says she's afraid of the dark, spritz some "Monster Repellent" in her room to calm her nerves. The repellent is really just cheap lavender body spray, but she won't know that.

Take turns dealing with your toddler at night so neither partner gets stuck with all the sleepless nights.

The biggest time suck of all, though, will come if you fall asleep waiting for her to fall asleep. Will it be nice to sleep? Yes, but it will also mean saying goodbye to your kid-free evening, and that is a punishment no parent deserves.

YOUR TODDLER THROUGH THE NIGHT

At last! Your toddler is asleep! That means you can finally relax and enjoy yourself, right? Well, sure, as long as you have an asterisk after that statement! The reality is that when you have a toddler you're never really off the clock. When a toddler goes down for the night, she's rarely down for long.

There are a lot of reasons your toddler will wake up at night. She might be thirsty and want a glass of water, she might need to go to the bathroom (usually a couple hours after she's asked for that glass of water), she might be cold and want you to pull up her covers (you know, the ones she kicked off herself), or she might have misplaced her favorite teddy bear (check under her pillow). Generally, getting your toddler back to sleep in these situations will be easy once you've addressed her need. The real challenge will come when your toddler has a nightmare.

The good news is that (if you keep your ears open and move quickly) you will often be able to stop a bad dream before it turns into a full-fledged nightmare. Hear some quiet whimpers coming from your toddler's room? If so, put down your wine and hustle back to your toddler's room! With a little luck, you'll be able to settle her with a few gentle rubs on the back. What you don't want

to do is try to drown out her whimpers by turning up the sound on the TV. Do that, and you'll likely end up watching a new show called *The Walking Dead—Toddler Edition*, and that's a show that can last well over an hour.

Some nights, though, there will be no stopping your toddler from waking up after a nightmare. When this happens, what should you do? This quiz should help you figure it out.

A) Comfort your toddler and then encourage independent sleeping by saying, "I will stand here in the doorway until you fall back to sleep."

B) Lie down with your toddler and let her fall back to sleep in your arms.

C) Bring your toddler into your bed to help her get back to sleep.

Ask parents which option is best, and most will say "A," but far fewer will actually do it in the middle of the night. Lying down with your kid is much easier, after all. But if you do that, she will expect you to lie down with her every time she has a nightmare. She may even start to pull the "I had a nightmare" con on a nightly basis to get those sweet, middle-of-the night cuddles.

The benefit of "C" is that it will allow your toddler to fall asleep quickly, which means that you will be able to fall asleep quickly too. The downside, though, is that you will be in bed with a toddler whose flying feet and flailing arms will do a number on you. Oh, and she will want to sleep with you again the next night. So, if you want your toddler to learn how to sleep on her own, you should limit how often you do this (or at least try). We realize it's easier said than done.

POTTY TRAINING SIGNS

Everyone will tell you that your toddler will show signs of "readiness" when she's ready to potty train. While that might seem ridiculous, it's actually true. You will need to keep an eye out for any signs that your toddler is ready to cooperate, because if you don't, you might find yourself slowly sliding down the bathroom wall, holding a diaper and crying, "I can't do it anymore!"

- Often the earliest sign is when your toddler starts to complain about being uncomfortable the second she uses her diaper. Instead of shouting, "Again?!" remind your toddler that a good way to not be uncomfortable is by letting you know before she uses her diaper. Start helping her identify the signals her body is sending.

- Your toddler will start wanting to watch you go to the bathroom. You might worry that your little one is showing the early signs of being a voyeur, but expressing an interest in other people's bodily functions is actually a totally normal sign that your toddler is moving toward being able to use the toilet.

- Toddlers who show flashes of "I do it myself!" independence are good potty training candidates. One of the ways toddlers express their autonomy is by removing their diapers. In typical toddler fashion, they do this partly because they can, and partly because they find it hilarious to watch their parents

SURVIVING BEDTIME AND POTTY TRAINING

run around like chickens with their heads cut off, desperate to get them back into another diaper. Don't get frustrated. Use their initiative to your advantage!

- If your toddler wakes up dry every morning, or goes for long, multi-hour stretches without needing a new diaper, her bladder muscles are likely getting stronger. Start keeping track of how many times your toddler wakes up dry (from overnight sleeping and naps). If she can string together several days in a row, she's definitely showing a sign she's ready to potty train.

In closing, the best way to know if your toddler is ready for potty training is by asking yourself if she's bribable. If she is, it's probably time. Toddlers, you see, don't really care about doing something for their own good—they want to do it for the candy (or the toy cars and stickers). Figure out your child's currency and then stock up. You'll want to be able to reward your toddler every single time she uses the toilet, so make sure to find something easy and cheap that will appeal to your toddler and not, say, a brand-new Barbie for every tinkle in the toilet.

METHODS OF POTTY TRAINING

The second you say the words "potty train," just about everyone you know (and some people you don't) will offer advice on which method you should use, solicited or not. Sure, Great Aunt Edna might have a suggestion, but it will require a chamber pot and access to a barn. Luckily, there are a variety of modern methods to potty train a toddler, and we've broken down the most popular ones so you can best determine what will work for your family.

The "Wait and Pee" Method: You place a kiddie potty in the bathroom, but never pressure your toddler to use it. You watch for signs that she needs to use the toilet, but never, you know, tell her to use it—you just hope she chooses to do it on her own.

PROS: There are fewer fights and fewer accidents. Your toddler will decide that going in the potty is her idea, which is especially good if she's headstrong and wants to do everything herself (this is 99 percent of all toddlers).

CONS: You will need to be the mellowest person on Earth because otherwise you might blow a gasket waiting for your toddler to "choose" to use the potty. Really, how long can you watch your toddler ignore the potty before you scream? It will be especially frustrating when you see your toddler take an interest in every single thing in your home except the freaking kiddie potty.

Training Pants Method: Disposable training diapers (which pull on and off like underwear, but are absorbent like diapers) can be used as you start potty training to help with the transition between diapers and underwear. You can even use "wet sensation" trainers that make the training pants especially uncomfortable when a child pees in them.

PROS: This is an in-between method that teaches your child how to pull her pants up and down and helps her avoid the trauma of peeing in her underwear. Accidents are much easier to clean up as well.

CONS: You're basically switching from one diaper to another, which means your toddler won't learn the full consequences of peeing in her pants. Even the wet sensation trainers might not be enough motivation to get your kid out of diapers and into underwear—after all, she's spent her entire life in diapers, so this won't be anything new.

Run Around Naked Method: You have your toddler run around the house naked for a few days, so that when she needs to pee there's no chance of her getting tangled up in her clothes. It will also make it easier for you to see the physical signs that she needs to use the toilet.

PROS: You won't have a mountain of underwear to wash, and getting your toddler onto the toilet when it's time to go will be much easier without clothes getting in the way.

CONS: Your child will be running around naked in your house, which means there's nothing containing any accident. Think about that for a second. So, yeah, you might not have a mountain of underwear to wash, but do you like shampooing rugs? Also, it's important that your toddler learns how to go to the bathroom with clothes on. Pulling down underwear is an important step in the potty training process.

Toilet in Front of the TV Method: You place a kiddie potty in front of the TV or in the family room where everyone hangs out. You then encourage your toddler to sit on the toilet for most of the day, making the toilet more familiar and comfortable.

PROS: This will show your toddler that the toilet isn't something to be afraid of (it's a surprisingly common fear). It will also reduce accidents because your kid will be sitting on the toilet for hours on end.

CONS: Sure, pooping in front of a TV is a dream for many, but it's best not to give your toddler unrealistic expectations about what being potty trained will be like. Plus, your living room will smell like crap, literally.

Three-Day Method: This is potty training boot camp. For three straight days, everyone stays home and focuses 100 percent on your toddler and her bathroom needs. Your kid will wear underwear and a shirt, and you must say, "Let me know when you have to go potty," every five minutes to signal to your toddler that she is the one in charge of her body.

PROS: If you're intense and do it right, you will (most likely) potty train your kid in three days. Your toddler will also learn how to read the signs her body is sending, so she will let you know when she needs to go without needing to be asked or reminded.

CONS: These three days will be some of the longest of your life. After two days of doing nothing but staring at your toddler's crotch, poised to race her into the bathroom, you might decide diapers are the lesser of two evils.

PUBLIC RESTROOMS

Just when you think you've survived the stress of potty training, you'll realize something terrifying—you're going to have to take your freshly potty-trained toddler out into the real world. Leaving the protective bubble of your home without the security of diapers will be very stressful, so much so that you may be the one with the urge to pee yourself! Yet as usual your toddler will be able to smell your fear. Since the last thing you want is for her to get nervous and forget everything she's learned, you must remain calm.

Start by putting some thought into your first trips out of the house with your potty-trained toddler. The goal should be short excursions, like walking over to the neighbor's house or a short drive to drop off dry cleaning. You'll want to make sure your child uses the bathroom before you go, and praise her like crazy if she stays dry on your entire trip out of the house. Anything you can do to help your child gain potty training confidence is a good thing.

In these early days, knowing where public restrooms are at all times is of the utmost importance as well. The last thing you want is to have to run through the aisles of the grocery store looking for the bathroom sign. A newly potty-trained toddler won't be able to hold her bladder for very long, and you don't want your kid to be responsible for a cleanup on aisle five. Instead, ask where the bathroom is as soon as you enter any building. Even if your toddler doesn't use the bathroom on that first trip, you never know when that information might come in handy.

Keep in mind that using a public toilet can be hard for a toddler. Public toilets are usually bigger (and look much different) than your toilets at home, and that can definitely intimidate or confuse the newly potty-trained. Stay positive and encouraging (even as your suddenly frantic toddler screams, "Nooooo!"), and help her maneuver this strange, new toilet. Bringing along a folding potty seat can be a big help in public restrooms too. (It may sound less than practical, but they often fold up small enough to fit into a purse or backpack.) Automatic flushing toilets are another hazard that can scare the literal crap out of your toddler. If the toilet has a sensor, make sure you cover it with your hand, toilet paper, or Post-it notes—anything that will keep it from triggering the toilet to flush.

Most of all, accept that your kid will probably have an accident in public and prepare for it. This means letting go of your dreams of leaving behind your diaper bag (for the time being at least). Stock it with extra clothes, wipes, paper towels, and other cleaning supplies. It's also smart to bring along a re-sealable plastic bag to stash wet clothes in. Once you're prepared for an accident, you'll be much more relaxed and ready to handle the inevitable.

TODDLER TIP #30

Little boys who stand to pee might not be tall enough to do this with a public toilet, but if you let him stand on your shoes he might be able to reach.

POTTY TRAINING PITFALLS

After you've made it through the worst parts of potty training, the last thing you'll want is for your toddler to regress. Yet parents are often the reason a potty-trained toddler backslides. Here are some pointers for lasting success:

- **Don't start too soon.** Did you see something on the Internet about infant potty training and freak out that you need to get moving? ("Oh no! My kid is eighteen months old and still in diapers! He'll never get into Harvard at this rate!") Well, don't. The reality is that there is no rush, and in all likelihood your kid won't graduate from college (Harvard or any other) in diapers. Wait until you're both ready. This isn't something you can force.

- **Once you start potty training your toddler, *do not stop.*** Your toddler will never figure out her body's signals if she still wears a diaper half the time. Yes, it will make your life easier if she wears a diaper on a long drive, but a few extra stops on a car trip will save you a lot of aggravation down the road.

- **Don't get angry when she has an accident.** Yes, you will want to scream when your toddler pees while sitting on your lap, but yelling will only make her think accidents are something to be hidden, and do you really want to have her start hiding soiled underwear around the house? (The answer is no. No, you do not.) Instead, speak calmly, remind her that she has to listen to her body, and then go change her clothes.

- **Potty training needs to be fun and interesting for your toddler.** If she figures out potty training is for her own good, she might lose interest. So, make sure you celebrate every victory with cheers and silly dances.

- **Keep the bribes/rewards regular, but simple.** If you keep upping the ante to get your toddler to pee in the potty, you're in trouble. Two or three M&Ms is a good reward, but a king-size bag of the chocolate candies is not.

- **Don't lose your resolve when things don't go according to plan.** Your child might not be potty trained by the last day of the Three-Day Method, but keep trying! Some kids take a little longer for everything to click and that's okay. Don't give up and lose the progress you've made. Have faith in your toddler and keep going.

PARENTAL
SELF-PRESERVATION

CHAPTER 9

When you're at war it's easy to lose morale and be overwhelmed by the direness of it all. It's why the United Service Organization (USO) exists—to send entertainers like Bob Hope and Marilyn Monroe (and Carrie Underwood in more recent years) overseas to give our troops a break and boost their morale. While the war you will find yourself locked in with a toddler will pale in comparison to the real deal, the same principle applies: you will need the occasional break too.

Hollywood celebrities are not going to show up at your home and perform a show to help get you through this. If you're going to make it to the other side of your kid's toddlerhood without losing it, you will need to find ways to give yourself a break now and again. So, take a deep breath and let it out slowly. Let's get through this together.

AFTER YOUR TODDLER GOES DOWN

Remember the euphoric feeling of walking out of school on the last day of the year? Well, that's a little like how you will feel each night once you finally get your toddler to sleep. You might even strut out of your toddler's room singing, "He's down for the night!" to the tune of Alice Cooper's "School's Out." And while you'll only have a couple hours off instead of a few months, you'll have many opportunities to make good and bad decisions.

One thing you'll definitely want to do is maximize your time. Since you'll be tired, it will be all too easy to plop down on the couch and just stare into space. Zoning out like this isn't the worst thing in the world, in fact, it could help you unwind, but you don't want to waste too much of your evening this way. Your toddler-free, adults-only time is fleeting!

So, if you spend your day longing to watch a TV show where the characters don't turn to the screen and ask questions, you should waste no time in dialing up those shows with swear words, shoot-outs, and doctors getting frisky with each other in broom closets (or all three at once). This would also be an ideal time to finally watch that Netflix series everyone is talking about, so you can actually chime in on conversations about it instead of having to shift the subject to the latest Netflix Original Series . . . for kids. ("Yeah, that detective show sounds great, guys, but you know what else is great? Netflix's new series about bugs that sing Beatles' songs! Hey, where are you going?")

If you're not into television but have a hobby that's meaningful to you, this is also a good time to do it. Whether it's writing, knitting, drawing, playing fantasy football, or making a paper mache statue of Steve Buscemi (hey, no judgment here), you will feel better having done it the next day when you're once again knee-deep in all things toddler.

This adults-only time will be a terrific opportunity to connect with your partner too. Talk to each other, cuddle, and joke around. Do the things you have a hard time doing when you're too busy stopping your toddler from eating things he finds on the ground or climbing onto counters. You and your partner may even choose to use this time to get frisky in your own broom closet, so to speak, but you shouldn't feel like you have to do it simply because this is a window of opportunity. After a long day of being toddlerized, you might be sweaty, exhausted, and not in the mood. If so, that's okay.

It should also be mentioned that it's perfectly fine to use this time to go to sleep. It may seem crazy to sleep away these precious hours, but if you're exhausted, sleep will replenish you a whole lot more than a couple hours of TV. Stock up on REM sleep, and you'll be much more likely to enjoy your toddler-free time the next night.

The one thing you absolutely must not do, though, is get carried away enjoying yourself and try to stretch this magical time out way longer than you should. You must have discipline; otherwise, you could come to your senses at 2:00 a.m. realizing you've binge-watched six episodes and polished off a bottle of wine. Make a mistake like that and you will hate life the next day (or even thirty minutes later when your toddler first cries out for you).

MAKING AN ESCAPE

Before you have kids, planning a date night is pretty damn easy. It's so easy, in fact, that people sometimes veto going out for the laziest of reasons, like, "Eh, we'd have to fill the car up with gas. Maybe just order in Chinese?" Once you have a toddler, though, going out becomes a lot more complicated. You've got to hire a babysitter, meticulously write out an information sheet (one that doesn't send your sitter running for her car), and steel yourself for your toddler's desperate pleas of "Don't go!" as you try to leave. But while arranging a date night might not be easy, you should do it anyway. Toddler-less trips into the real world are incredibly important for you, your partner, and your relationship.

The best reason to have a date night is because it will remind you of why you started your family in the first place. You might be thinking, "How could I ever forget why I started my family?" But when you're knee-deep in all things toddler, you and your partner can start to feel like you're nothing more than coworkers at *Toddler, Inc.*, a company that specializes in keeping your crazy toddler from doing harm to himself and others. As coworkers at this start-up, the majority of your interactions will involve changing diapers, cutting up grapes, and tag-teaming the bedtime routine. You will also find yourself shouting romantic things at each other like, "Can you please take the toddler?! I have to go die in the bathroom from this stomach bug!" Do this long enough and it's all too easy to forget that you actually really enjoy each other's company and conversations about things other than

baby gates. This is why date nights are so key—they give you the perfect opportunity to talk like you used to.

In a way, they can kind of feel like a first date: You: "Wow! You know a lot about history! Impressive! Did I know that about you?"

Your partner: "Yes, but before the toddler. And you have such a great sense of humor! I think I sort of remember that about you!"

Date nights are also a terrific way for you and your partner to see each other in something other than sweatpants and old, toddler food–stained T-shirts. So, take the opportunity to shower, groom yourself, and dress up! You'll feel better and your partner will be impressed (and vice versa).

One thing you don't want to do is to make these dates all about your kid. ("I can't believe he's walking already. We really should stop at Babies 'R' Us on the way home to get stuff to babyproof the cabinets . . . ") Sure, talking about your toddler a little bit is fine. But you shouldn't do it the whole time, since you'll have plenty of time to discuss him when you're back on the clock at *Toddler, Inc.*

You should also avoid constantly calling and texting home to check up on your toddler. Instead, be present with your partner and enjoy your chemistry. Hold hands, steal a few kisses, and take cheesy selfies together! Do enough of that, and by the end of night things might even progress to this point:

Your partner: "I'm really feeling you, and I know this might be a little complicated since we work together, but—"
You: "Wait. You do realize we don't actually work together, right?"

Your partner: "We don't?"

You: "No, we're married."

Your partner: "That's right! Score!"

Ideally, you will return home after your date recharged and feeling closer than ever—at least until your toddler poops his diaper and starts screaming for a toy you haven't seen in six months.

SEEING FRIENDS

Seeing your friends will go a long way toward helping you get through these toddler years. In case you need a reminder, your friends are the people who know the "old" you: the you who can never pick a song in the right key at karaoke, the you who is an expert in something fairly pointless (*Friends* trivia, cat memes), and the you who has talents well beyond diaper changing. They know you as more than "Toddler's Parent," and while you may love being known as "Toddler's Parent," there are other aspects of your identity you will want to keep in touch with too.

Of course, now that you and your friends are adults, it's much harder to hang out spontaneously. Gone are the "let's meet at the bar in twenty minutes" texts. Now spending

continued on page 180

TODDLER TIP #31

Set up a recurring, monthly get-together with your friends. It will ensure you make the time for each other.

RECORDED TODDLER DYSFUNCTION THROUGHOUT HISTORY

While today's worldwide epidemic of toddler dysfunction is unlike any other in history, there have been nine recorded clusters of extremely unruly toddlers. The last cluster that was in Hawthorne, California, between the years of 1956 and 1959 inspired one entrepreneur to start a business called "Toodles, Toddler." The following radio spot (transcribed below) gives fascinating insight into this difficult time:

CLIENT: "Toodles, Toddler"
LENGTH: Sixty seconds
MEDIUM: Radio

>   SOUND: A two-year-old wails as things SHATTER throughout the entirety of the spot.

>   WOMAN: Golly gee, am I exhausted!

>   MAN: Aw shucks, honey. The toddler just broke the television. Again. Rats!

>   MAN #2: You two look like you could use a night out.

>   MAN: Who are you? And what are you doing in our home?

>   MAN #2: I let myself in. It's the fifties. We do things like that. So, how's that night out sound?

>   WOMAN: A night out sounds swell, but no babysitter in town will watch our toddler.

MAN #2: Then bring him with you.

MAN: Not a chance, daddy-o. He's been banned from every restaurant in town.

MAN #2: Not every restaurant. The newly opened Toodles, Toddler caters specifically to the parents of incredibly frustrating two- and three-year-olds like yours. When you arrive, we will take your toddler and place him in a soundproof, padded room where he will remain safely while you enjoy your meal . . . in peace.

WOMAN: I don't know if I remember how to do that!

MAN #2: That's why we seat an interesting non-parent at every table to help our guests enjoy conversation about things other than diaper changes and tantrums.

MAN: Wow! Could he explain to me what the deal is with this Elvis character?

MAN #2: You bet, hound dog! So come on down to 435 El Segundo and let us lock your toddler in a padded room! He won't mind, and you deserve it!

time with your friends requires a major scheduling effort. Business trips, spouses, and children's activities all have to be taken into consideration. Finding a time that works will be hard, but it's worth the effort. If you don't try to make it happen, it never will.

There are some pitfalls you'll want to avoid when you're finally with your friends. For example, it might be hard to turn off "Mom" or "Dad" mode, especially since you play that role every second of the day. But the last thing you want to do is be the buzzkill who interrupts every fun story with an anecdote about your toddler's potty-training woes. You also don't want to ask your friends if they need to "go potty," and they definitely don't need you to wipe their mouths after they take a particularly messy bite of dinner. Do these things enough and eventually someone in your circle will say, "I love Marci and all, but . . ." Don't be Marci.

You should also spend time with your friends focusing on your relationships and the things you used to do. You don't have to worry about the kids at home—they're fine. Be present with your friends, laugh, say crazy things, and enjoy yourself. These are the moments that you'll cling to during your toddler's next bout of explosive diarrhea.

This isn't to say that you shouldn't talk about your kids at all—your friends will want to hear about your precious little monster, and they'll definitely want to know how you're handling life as a parent. Your friends love you, and being with them will give you a great opportunity to blow off steam. You can safely discuss your mistakes (like how your toddler dropped an F-bomb in the library) or admit you're so frustrated with things that you're thinking of selling your toddler. You can't say these things to your child's librarian, but you can say them to your friends. They'll make you feel better about your mistakes, talk you down off the ledge, and offer advice about what worked for them in similar situations. And, if they can see that you're really serious about selling your toddler, your friends will even help you write a really kickass Craigslist post. After all, that's what friends are for.

MINI-VACATIONS

In a perfect world, you would be able to recharge by taking bimonthly, government-funded trips to Hawaii without your toddler. In the world we actually live in, the best you can try for is what we call "mini-vacations," also known as brief, stolen moments when your toddler isn't hanging on you or whining for something to eat. If you hope to make it to the end of your kid's toddlerhood with your wits intact, you absolutely must learn how to make the most of these mini-vacations.

The first thing you'll need to do is recognize when these moments are happening because at first they'll be all too easy to let slip by unnoticed. For example, few parents of toddlers think of the time they spend filling their cars up

TODDLER TIP #32 If you're lucky enough to wake before your toddler, avoid making loud noises that might alert the toddler to the fact that you're up.

with gas as a chance to relax, but they (and you) should. Why? Because for that minute or so you will be outside of your car while your toddler will be inside of it. This means that as long as the gas keeps flowing you're 100 percent on "you" time! To unwind, take a nice, deep breath (but not too deep on account of all the gas fumes), and entertain yourself by watching the cars zoom by. Another great way to amuse yourself is by pretending you're on a game show called *Guess How Much It Will Cost To Fill Up Your Tank!* ("I guess thirty-one dollars, Chuck! Thirty-one! Let me see big thirty-one!") Make the most of this time, and when you slide back behind the wheel (and hear your toddler whining in the back), you will feel just a bit fresher.

There will be many more moments like this that you will need to be on the lookout for. If your toddler runs off to harass your partner as he or she tries to use the bathroom, you're on "you time!" If your toddler opens a new toy and actually engages with it for a minute or two, you're on "you time!" If you somehow wake up before your toddler, you're definitely on "you time!"

If you become adept at recognizing these moments, you will start to see more and more of them every day. And while you will eventually be able to take a vacation somewhere more exciting than the gas station, in the meantime these mini-vacations will be all you've got, so you'd best enjoy them.

ALONE TIME

Remember the classic power ballad that went, "All by myself, don't want to be . . . all by myself?" Well, that's one song you never sing when you have a toddler because you'll freaking love being alone.

Now you might be thinking, "You don't have to remind me to enjoy alone time," but the reality is that once you have a toddler you can actually forget how to be alone. It's all too easy to end up wasting your alone time by cleaning the house or folding your toddler's tiny laundry instead of reading a book (remember that?). Those chores will need to get done,

TODDLER TIP #33

Try arranging alone time swaps with your partner. Take an hour or two by yourself one day, then let your partner have the same amount of time the next day.

of course, but when you have alone time it's important for your mental well-being that you use it for yourself.

It's also smart to use this time to do things you normally have to do with your toddler, only solo. For example, this will be your chance to use the restroom without your toddler leaning on your knee and flushing the toilet over and over. You will also be able to make yourself some food and eat it without having to share every other bite. Even better, you will be able to gorge on candy without having to hide in the bathroom and yell through the door, "I'll be right out, sweetie! Just eating this Twix—er, I mean, washing my hands!"

There will also be glorious times when you get to run errands alone because your partner or someone else is watching your toddler. On those occasions it will be easy to slip into "super fast-forward racing through the store with a toddler mode," but it's important to remind yourself you are *not* with your toddler. You can actually slow down and shop like a normal human being! Want to inspect the strawberries instead of hurriedly tossing the first carton you can grab into the cart like you're on *Supermarket Sweep?* Then do it! You can even go crazy and compare prices! You'll be glad you did the next time you're at the market and your toddler is pulling cereal boxes off the shelf.

PARENTAL SELF-PRESERVATION

AFTERMATH:
TRANSITIONING INTO POST-TODDLER LIFE

After forty days and forty nights of torrential rain, Noah awoke on his ark one morning to discover that it had at last stopped raining. He saw the sun was out, that there was a rainbow on the horizon, and in that moment realized that the worst was behind him. Like Noah, you too will wake one morning to discover a very different world than you were used to. When you tell your child "no," she won't flop onto the floor and kick her feet. When you go to the bathroom, she won't follow you in there and unspool the toilet paper roll. And when you eat a piece of cheese, she won't reach for it with her sticky, little hands and screech, "Mine!" Will your child suddenly be a total angel? No, of course not. She will now be a preschooler (they come with

187

their own set of problems), but the worst will be behind you. You will have emerged from the Toddler Wars triumphant!

Moving forward won't be so simple, however. You will have spent a long time adjusting to life with a toddler, and letting go of it may prove difficult. Many suffer from POFT (Parents of Former Toddlers) disorder. They continue to only eat out at fast food restaurants long after their kid is able to handle something a little more formal. Other sufferers still wake in the night humming that Elmo song. In order to live freely again, you must let go of these things. If you don't, the toddlers will have won!

Ironically, once you do finally leave your kid's toddlerhood in the past, it will likely start to seem like nothing but a bad dream. Your memories will grow hazy, and you'll question whether the worst of it actually happened. You'll think, "I seem to have a memory of my toddler peeing in the mall fountain in front of hundreds of horrified people, but that couldn't have happened, could it? No, I must have seen that on television."

In most instances, forgetting these traumas will be healthy, but it can be dangerous too. Forget what a toddler is really like, and you may make the mistake of agreeing to babysit someone's toddler. You may even decide to have another child (a.k.a. a future toddler) without giving it the proper consideration. Deciding to have another toddler should only be done with a clear-headed understanding of what you will have to endure once again. (Re-reading this survival guide is one way you can properly reacquaint yourself with the realities of toddlerhood.)

Finally, we would be remiss in our duties if we failed to acknowledge that no one knows what awaits humankind if this epidemic of extreme toddler dysfunction continues. While it's possible this scourge will run its course (and toddlers will return to being the midlevel troublemakers they'd been for thousands of years) toddlerologists warn that toddlers may grow even more unruly and advanced in their mischief. If that happens and tomorrow's toddlers make today's look like sweet little cherubs . . . well, it's best that we don't even contemplate it.

For now, the only ill-behaved toddler you will have to contend with is your own. We hope this handbook serves you well. Godspeed, parents.

INDEX

ABOUT THE AUTHORS

Mike Spohr is the founding editor of
BuzzFeed Parents. **Heather Spohr**
writes the popular parenting website
The Spohrs Are Multiplying.
Graduates of the University of
Southern California, they live
in Los Angeles, where they
survived the toddler wars
with their kids.

ACKNOWLEDGMENTS

Mike: I would like to thank my parents, Anthony and Kathy Spohr,
for their unending support (and for taking me to at least one
hundred San Francisco Giants games as a kid). Thanks also to Erin
La Rosa and Peggy Wang of BuzzFeed, for their professional support.

Heather: I would like to thank my parents, Kirk and Linda
Buchanan, for always encouraging and supporting my dreams
(and for babysitting while I try to achieve them!). I'd also like
to thank my grandmother, Mary Alice, for the confidence she
instilled in me and for her love.

Together we'd like to thank our editor, Thom O'Hearn, for his
guidance, as well as James Kegley, Caitlin Fultz, Ted Slampyak, and
the rest of the book's team. Last but not least: thanks to our kids,
Madeline, Annabel, and James. (Annabel, by the way, would like you
to know she "wrote a couple of the jokes" in this book, which is true!)